[handwritten: Henry K____]

[handwritten: February 2nd (weak shadow today.]

Acknowledgements

Although writing this book was a solitary effort I must acknowledge those people who were most helpful along the way.

In the early stages, Writer-in-Residence at the University of Alberta, Myrna Kostash, tidied up the English of some sample drafts and who, in a moment of inspiration, suggested that I add the term "Secrets of Great Slave Lake" as sub-title to my book.

Posthumously I would be remiss not to mention the encouragement given by Helen Christensen, our late office secretary, who kept bringing me up to date on related adventures involved in searching for sunken equipment.

Thanks to my engineering friend George Faulder for removing the mysteries as to the temperature of steam under normal atmospheric pressure as compared to when confined under higher pressures. Also to Architect and former Pilot Jack Gardener for clarifying why Northern pilots prefer to navigate by gyro-compass instead of by magnetic compass. And, at the end, manuscripts must be typed and for doing this task I am grateful to Anne Margaret Wall for her prompt and excellent work.

Library and Archives Canada Cataloguing in Publication

Copyright © Henry Kasten, 2004

Published by the Author, Henry Kasten
            9012 – 142 St. N.W., Edmonton, AB T5R 0M5
            Tel: 780.483.8255

Kasten, Henry, 1923-
            The Captain's Course : Secrets of Great Slave Lake /
            Henry Kasten

Includes bibliographical references.

ISBN 0-9736641-0-X

    1. Great Slave Lake (N.W.T.) — History.
    2. Salvage — Northwest Territories — Great Slave Lake — History.
    3. Shipwrecks — Northwest Territories — Great Slave Lake — History.
    I. Title.

FC4195.G75K37 2004   971.9 ' 203   C2004-906173-9

The Captain's Course

DEDICATION

I dedicate this book to our youngest children, Mary and Gerry, who were too young to understand what their Dad was up to in their early years.

AUTHOR'S ERRATA:
P69,L16 DELETE 'EACH'
P114,L7SEND, NOT SENT

THE CAPTAIN'S COURSE: SECRETS OF GREAT SLAVE LAKE

CONTENTS

PART EIGHT   **APPENDICES**

Appendix 1: Figure 1, Harry's
Strong Signal

Appendix 2: Steamship Inspector's
Report

Appendix 3: Figure 3, Agreement for
finding Steel Barge

Appendix 4: Photographs

Appendix 5: Maps

Appendix 6: Glossary of Terms

Appendix 7: Table of Selected
Equivalents

Appendix 8: Bibliography

PREFACE

The main events of this story took place during the period from 1940 to 1980 in the domain of the very large Great Slave Lake in the western sub-arctic region of Canada. In view of this it may be helpful to set down certain terms relating to direction and measurement that were common to the area and to the time.

For direction, the common instrument on the lake was the Magnetic Compass. This meant that the direction North was taken as the direction to which the compass needle pointed at any location. The needle points towards the North Magnetic Pole which is located hundreds of miles to the east of the true North Pole. In the locale described in this book the needle pointed in a direction some 32 degrees east of true north. This was called **NORTH** and if a relationship to True North was required then one would refer to navigation charts giving the deviation of the needle at various locations. One major exception to this convention occurs in most airplanes flying in the area which, as a rule, have both a magnetic compass and a gyro-compass. The latter indicates the true north direction and holds a course much more steadily than a magnetic compass.

The major part of this story took place before 1970, the year that metrication began to be introduced in Canada, including the Celsius scale of temperatures. In our search procedures we were continuously using the Imperial System of measurements including the Fahrenheit scale. I realize that a whole generation of Canadians has grown up since 1970 and become fluent in the use of the metric system. As I started writing this book I began to set down, in brackets, the metric equivalent to each Imperial Term. However, these were so many and so frequent, I felt that the interruptions to the flow of the text would be annoying. My decision early on was to retain Imperial terminology exclusively and provide a table of equivalents to cover the most significant measurements given.

PART ONE: "MAC AND MAC" STEEPLEJACK

In mid-summer, 1959, a small steeplejack company moved from Toronto to Edmonton. The firm consisted of two principals, Claud McDonald and Don McCallum, one employee, Eddie LeBlanc, and a one-ton panel truck lightly loaded with miscellaneous rigging equipment. It specialized in servicing tall broadcasting towers in general and particularly guyed towers as opposed to free standing. By August they had won a contract for re-painting the broadcast tower of CFRN Television at the western outskirts of Edmonton. This tower had been erected in 1954 which is the year that this station became Edmonton's first private television broadcaster.

For aircraft safety tall towers must be painted to a distinctive pattern of alternating bands of White and International Orange colors. The rule of thumb at the time was to repaint every five years so as to keep the colors bright. Thus CFRN, being a good corporate citizen, invited tenders for repainting the tower in the summer of '59 and in this Mac and Mac were successful in winning the job.

Now it so happened that I had carried out a small assignment of professional work on the tower in the year of its erection, mainly in certifying the structural adequacy of the concrete used in its foundation. This may have been the reason our firm received a request from CFRN to inspect the painting work as it was being carried out, eventually to certify the quality of the materials and workmanship. This involved a few trips to the site to inspect the paints supplied and the rate and evenness of application. This was Eddie Leblanc's job who clambered over the tower framework with speed and agility to carry out his duties. I found the workmanship to be entirely satisfactory and so advised our client.

During the next month or two I met occasionally with McDonald and McCallum, once actually climbing up to a church steeple with McCallum to advise him on his preparation of a bid on a tendered contract for repairing the steeple.

Although the Mac and Mac business did not appear to be prospering, the association between us continued and soon developed into a friendly relationship. As I began to know them better I realized that the two principals were of quite different temperaments.

McDonald, although the younger of the two, was the technical strength of the pair. In his early thirties he was, in addition to being an experienced rigger and member of the Ironworkers Union, a capable diver with both hard-helmet and Scuba experience. He was blunt in his speech, giving the impression of a no-nonsense approach to any task at hand. McCallum was older, also a member of the Ironworkers Union, and the diplomat of the two. He possessed good negotiating and mediating abilities and, surprisingly enough, was openly and justifiably proud of admitting that he was a reformed alcoholic. In spite of these differences the two got along well and formed a good partnership.

About this time, in fact before winter, the two took me into their confidence and revealed that, in reality, a unique event lay behind their reason for moving to Edmonton. They had decided to use Edmonton as their base from which to launch a search for a lost shipment of new Caterpillar Tractors that lay scattered on the bottom of Great Slave Lake in the Northwest Territories.

I had never heard of this loss, likely because the event had taken place seventeen years earlier in 1942. Claud and Don, seeing that I appeared skeptical, suggested that I read the September 1945 issue of the Beaver Magazine which gives a detailed account of the loss.

PART TWO: THE MISHAP

In 1942 construction of the Canol Pipeline in the Northwest Territory of Canada was well into its early stages. This project was being built as part of the war effort of the United States. The 4-inch pipe would transport crude oil from the Norman Wells oilfield on the Mackenzie River across the Mackenzie Mountains to an oil refinery at Whitehorse, Yukon Territory. Here the crude would be refined to gasoline for refueling warplanes flying the Northwest Staging Route. All of this was in preparation to answer the possibility of Japanese aggression against Alaska.

Completion of the pipeline project was under the direction of the U.S. Army but the actual construction work was subcontracted to a consortium of nine American firms established under the name of Bechtel, Price, Callaghan, called the Constructor.

Although the construction was located deep in the Northwest Territory, at approximate latitude 65 degrees North, not far from the Arctic Circle, there existed a water transportation route feasible all summer for delivering heavy construction material to Norman Wells. This was the inland shipping route along the Mackenzie River system. This began at the railhead of Waterways, Alberta, which was the northern terminal of the Northern

Alberta Railway originating at Edmonton. At the small village of Waterways a staging area was available on the banks of the Clearwater River for loading freight onto barges which could be assembled into barge trains to be pulled by tug-boats onto the Athabasca River leading eventually to the Mackenzie River.

In early spring, 1942, Bechtel, Price, Callaghan were busy at Waterways acquiring and building barges for transporting freight and equipment to Norman Wells. The shipping season would not open until late May or early June because the portion of the water route which passes across Great Slave Lake would be blocked by ice until that time.

In due course a number of barges were loaded and assembled behind a tug-boat ready for towing to Norman Wells. This was a major shipment of heavy construction equipment consisting of six 20-ton Caterpillar bulldozer tractors and two road graders. In addition there were substantial quantities of oil, gasoline, spare parts and provisions resulting in a total shipment valued at a quarter million dollars.

The route ahead would follow a course that had been used by river vessels since the turn of the century: Down the Athabasca River past the west end of Lake Athabasca, then down the Slave River towards Great Slave Lake. However, the Slave

River presented a major navigational obstacle in the form of twenty miles of impassible rapids beginning at Fitzgerald and ending at Fort Smith. Here, over the years, a portage roadway had been constructed which was adequate for moving boats, barges and freight by heavy tractor-trailer transport around the rapids, to be re-assembled on smooth water at Fort Smith. The final stage of the journey would be down the remainder of the Slave to Great Slave Lake, across the western end of the lake to its outflow into the Mackenzie River and down the Mackenzie to Norman Wells. The total length of water travel would be some 1,100 miles.

Near mid-July of 1942 the tug PROSPECTOR and its train of barges put in at the village of Fort Resolution located on Great Slave Lake at the western edge of the Slave River Delta. This village, with a history of 200 years as a fur trading post, has a small harbour and is a logical stopping point for vessels before entering the lake. The Captain was facing a crossing of some 120 miles of open water before reaching the Mackenzie.

As he prepared to leave, it seems that the Captain experienced a sense of foreboding that a storm was brewing. He mentioned his concern to the U.S. Army Colonel who was accompanying the PROSPECTOR on its trip. Nevertheless, possibly because of an urgency in schedule, a decision was taken to proceed.

The Captain's Course

The course begins as a two-mile section to just south of Round Island and then branches into three separate choices: An open water course directly to the start of the Mackenzie; an alternative course just outside a group of several islands in Resolution Bay heading to an intermediate stop at Hay River some 65 miles down the lake; or, the track usually followed, passing between the islands on the way to Hay River. It is clear that the Captain chose the course just outside the islands, possibly to avoid unmarked Pilot Reef lying between Burnt and Green Islands and known to be just a few feet beneath summer water level.

By late afternoon the barge train had reached an area about 20 miles from Resolution, somewhat past Burnt Island, the largest of the group of islands. At this point the Captain's premonition became a reality. With little forewarning a furious summer storm bore down across the lake from the north-west. In this area north-west winds have a reach of some 60 miles across open water and the size of the waves can be legendary. During one similar storm in the sixties, in the same general area, a Fisheries ship was driven past the shore line and deposited on land within the spruce trees that grow down to the fringe of the shore.

The flotilla was soon in serious trouble. Buffeted by high waves, the clumsy barges would be severely tilted and cargo would be falling off. Although at this latitude and time of year daylight lasts until 11 p.m., it is uncertain, considering the storm, whether the Captain would be able to see what the state of the barges was. The Beaver article states that the Captain decided to cut the tow line. However, subsequent events prove that instead the Captain decided to turn the flotilla around and head for shelter at Burnt Island.

Every Captain in the area would know about the haven of Burnt Island. This island, close to shipping routes, has two sheltering bays, one facing generally west and the other facing generally east. There is a narrow neck of land, only some two hundred yards wide, between the two bays. A mature spruce forest covers the neck, thereby providing a good wind break. The east bay is known as an anchorage and the Captain would head for this to be in lee of the west wind.

The Captain successfully reached the east bay. Only then, it appears, were the barges cut free. The next day the Captain found all the barges washed up on the south shore of the lake, bare of all cargo. That same day the two road graders were found in shallower water near the south tip of Burnt, where the exhaust pipes of the graders were seen to be projecting about 6 inches above water.

PART THREE: THE RESEARCH COUNCIL SEARCH
Phase One: September and October, 1942

The loss of the six Bulldozers would have been a severe blow to the scheduled construction of the pipeline in the summer of 1942. Evidently quite quickly after the accident the Bechtel, Price, Callaghan group were investigating possible measures for recovery of the tractors. In early September the National Research Council of Canada received an urgent request from BPC as to whether it could assist in finding the sunken tractors.

The Research Council did have two young scientists on staff who had developed a device they called a Magnetic Gradiometer. This had been designed to detect submerged iron objects and, since it was wartime, one would think that submarines were the intended target. The Council immediately assigned one of the scientists, Dr. Claud Kitchener Jones, age 25 and hailing from Regina, to initiate a search that fall in conjunction with the U.S. Army.

Aided by Army forces, Claud Jones and his magnetic device reached Ft. Resolution in late September. He was provided with a self-propelled barge and several helpers. In Resolution a steel barge carrying a tracked tractor was added, to be towed by the motorized barge. On a calm day in early October, Claud Jones and his crew made an uneventful trip across Resolution Bay to Burnt Island. This would be their base for a late autumn water search.

After anchoring in the east bay and retiring for the night, the men were awakened about three hours later by heavy waves pounding on the beach. A strong storm had come from the east and was threatening the safety of the barges. A decision was made to release the towed barge and very soon thereafter the men saw this barge beach itself on the shore of the bay.

It was then decided to cruise around the island with the motorized barge to find a sheltered area. They circumnavigated for the remainder of the night and all of the next day but there was no let-up in wind although the direction of the blow varied. Worse still a heavy rain was now falling. Somewhere on the far side of the island the men anchored the barge close to shore. Leaving one man on the barge the rest used a rowboat to get back to land. They then continued to circle the island on foot and eventually returned to the east bay, finding the other barge still safely beached. Thereupon they drove the tractor down onto the island and ran it across the island to the anchored barge. A line was gotten on board and the tractor was able to pull the barge safely onto land.

For the next several days the rain continued, quite unusual for October. Blustery winds carried on thus precluding getting a water search under way.

It was now well into October and within a few days ice sheets began to form on the lake. Reluctantly Claud Jones decided that the idea of an autumn search must be abandoned. Therefore he returned to home base intent on making preparations for a winter search.

Phase Two: The Search Completed, 1943

In his official report Jones stated that by 15 February, 1943, the instrument was ready for transport. Then, by March 14, a search on the ice was ready to proceed. By that time it was felt that the ice would be thick enough to carry the heavy equipment that had been assembled. This consisted of the tractor that had been left on the island, two haulage trucks, three cabooses for accommodation of the crew and the magnetic detection device. The crew consisted of six men: C.K. Jones, Director, and local men Gordon Greenway, former trapper, Dave Lent, George Clarke, Art Dionne and Alex Bentman. The detecting device was in the care of Jones who also brought with him a sketch map prepared by the Captain showing his estimate of the course followed on his retreat to Burnt Island. Based on the Captain's sketch, Jones estimated that the ideal area to be searched would comprise a rectangle some 4 miles wide by 8 miles long, that is, 32 square miles in all.

After several days of experimenting a practical search procedure was developed. The Magnetic Detector, usually called "The Head", was towed on a sled some 60 feet behind a caboose, connected to it by an electric cable. The caboose was towed by the tractor and was large enough to carry all electronic equipment and also serve as sleeping quarters for the crew. The equipment consisted of the detector on the sled, an amplifier which strengthened the signals from the detector, and an Esterline-Angus recorder to mark the signals as permanent ink lines on a moving and timed strip of graph paper and two twenty four volt wet-cell batteries providing direct current power for operating the entire detection assemblage. The range of the detector head had been designed as 50 feet and eventually Jones found that it could be somewhat more than 50 feet.

To understand the operation of the detection system one must visualize that the entire sphere of the earth is constantly surrounded by invisible curvi-linear magnetic lines of force connecting the two magnetic poles of the earth. Under normal conditions these lines of force move more or less uniformly although with small erratic variations. The coils of the detector head align themselves with the magnetic lines of force. Under these conditions the signals are recorded on the paper strip as slightly irregular wavy lines. If a large iron object is present the magnetic lines are strongly directed towards it because iron has a strong magnetic attraction. This sudden change of direction of the lines is recorded on the paper as a sharply peaked line, i.e. a change in gradient or slope of the magnetic lines, hence the term Gradiometer.

When the search began there were two feet of snow on the ice, rather more than normal. It was found necessary to first clear roadways with the tractor. A straight cleared trail would be run for a mile and then a parallel return trail would be run about 30 feet over. The search assembly would be pulled along the trails at some two to three miles per hour, then the procedure was repeated.

In addition to the snow the lake presented other formidable obstacles. The most general were large areas of rough ice. These develop when high winds blow across the lake in the early days after freeze up. Ice 6 to 8 inches thick may break up and be driven before the wind into a random jumble and then freeze in place, impassable to wheels and sleigh runners.

The Captain's Course

Shrinkage cracks and pressure ridges can develop into irregular barriers across the ice to interfere with travel. These develop from temperature swings at the surface of the huge areas of ice on the lake. When severe cold spells occur the ice contracts and opens up wide cracks exposing open water. This freezes firm but when a spell of relatively warm temperature returns the ice sheet expands and buckles, usually along the former cracks. This can create ice ridges in the order of ten feet high. The Jones crew ran into its share of such obstacles and in one case was able to pass through an ice ridge at a crossing cut through a ridge by Bechtel, Price, Callaghan to facilitate their freighting operations across the lake.

The search progressed slowly. After more than a week of searching without any signal from the detector, a certain amount of skepticism developed among the crew. Upon sensing this Jones decided on a showdown. He instructed George Clarke to take a number of heavy iron pipe wrenches and an axe, then go out on the lake and chop a hole in the ice to conceal them. When George came back Claud instructed him to drive around and, within the next 15 minutes, to go near the spot where he had buried the iron. After a while George drove near the hidden cache and, looking back, watched for a signal from the caboose. Suddenly he saw a block of wood fly out of the caboose window and land within a few feet of the cache. There was a cheer from the rest of the crew when they realized that science had won.

The work continued. On March 24th Jones recorded that they were plowing through about eighty acres a day. That is not a bad rate as it represents searching a quarter square mile of surface in two days.

The break came on March 27th when Jones recorded a beautiful signal that checked on each of several passes over the same area. On March 31st, after a few hold-ups in 30 degrees below Fahrenheit weather, they dug a hole in the ice and, leaving a thin bottom to the hole, were able to see the seat of a Caterpillar tractor. This showed how accurately Jones had maneuvered the detector as he finalized his reading as to the location of the iron.

While the crew began the task of raising the tractor, Jones carried on searching in the same general area. Surprisingly he got another signal the very next day. This, however, turned out to be a 300 pound sea anchor which, after two days of effort, was brought to the surface. The reason for its existence remains a mystery. It does seem appropriate that it was found just outside the east bay which has become known as the Anchorage. This anchor was found most useful in raising the tractor.

Searching continued until April 13th by which time rough ice and flooding due to spring melt waters were slowing things down. On April 16th searching operations ended. Two days later Jones was able to obtain passage on a U.S. Army plane going west that made an unscheduled stop at Resolution. The flight took him over Burnt Island and he could see a large timber tripod over a hole in the ice. Over to one side was the tractor. He saw one of the men jump on the driver's seat and run the salvaged tractor around in circles.

It is said that the Research Council received ten thousand dollars for the tractor, a sum which essentially paid the cost of the search.

In planning the next search Claud Jones felt that a summer search using a number of motor boats each carrying a detector would have a good likelihood of finding the other tractors. He quickly presented his idea to the U.S. Army. However, the urgency seemed to have passed and the result was that no further search was carried out by the authorities.

As a true scientist, Jones prepared an official report to the Research Council outlining the search carried out on behalf of Bechtel, Price, Callaghan. The report is titled "Magnetic Detection of Lost Objects" and presents a dispassionate account of the science involved and the results achieved. It was issued on 25 May, 1943 and was labeled

SECRET. It was declassified on February 15, 1957.

Considering the equipment used it is my opinion that the search was a well executed operation. Finding one cat demonstrated the feasibility of locating the invisible tractor in the huge, rather featureless unmarked area. Where the Cat was found, just outside the sheltered east anchorage of Burnt, vindicated Jones' stated analysis that there were two places where the Cats would be most likely to be found: where the flotilla was broadside to the west wind and that would be when the Captain first turned to retreat to Burnt and secondly when he finally turned to enter the sheltered east anchorage. And the obvious conclusion to be drawn from the location of the found Cat is that the tow line was not cut during the retreat towards Burnt Island.

PART FOUR: THE "MAC AND MAC" SEARCHES
Phase One: December, 1959 and January 1960

Following the Research Council search there were sporadic attempts by local searchers usually working out of the town of Hay River on the south shore of the lake. In his book "The Mysterious North" Pierre Berton, telling of his trip on a tugboat on Great Slave Lake in August, 1954, comments as follows: *"On Great Slave Lake a boat with two men hove briefly into view and then was swallowed up again, a vanishing speck on the vast leaden sheet of lonely water. These men were part of a crew helping to salvage tractors lost in the storms during the wartime construction of the great Canol oil pipeline."* In part V of the book Berton elaborates a bit more about losses by sinkings in the vicinity of Burnt Island.

After 1942 it would be seventeen years before another extensive attempt was made to find the lost Cats. Late in 1959, Claud McDonald and Don McCallum were busy putting together plans to carry out a winter search by air. As members of the local Ironworker's Union, they had ample opportunity to acquaint their Union buddies with their plan to search for lost tractors. Evidently such a venture appealed to the Ironworkers as

Mac and Mac had no difficulty in obtaining pledges of support, both in financing and participation.

With help of their connections in the East, Mac and Mac were able to rent a Magnetometer from a Mr. Johnson in Toronto. By this time a commercial version had been developed embodying the principles of the C.K. Jones' Magnetic Gradiometer. Rental would be on a monthly basis and would include the detecting head. It would be possible to carry out an aerial search using a small airplane flying over ice or water at low altitude.

The magnetometer did pose one problem for Mac and Mac in that they did not know a person with electronic training to operate the device. They turned to the University of Alberta for help. Through that connection a man with the necessary experience was found from outside the University. This was Harry Hubbard, an electronics technician who had received his training while enlisted in the Royal Canadian Air Force. He had subsequently worked for the Halliburton Oil Company on electronic logging of oil wells and eventually operated his own electronics servicing shop. Harry was contacted by Don McCallum and, evidently intrigued by the novelty of the proposed venture, agreed to become the magnetometer operator.

On December 20, 1959, a party consisting of McDonald, McCallum, Hubbard and ironworkers

The Captain's Course

Don Hicks and Guy Tiepel left Edmonton for Great Slave Lake. They arrived in Hay River N.W.T. on December 22nd after driving some 600 miles over the Mackenzie Highway, completed as a gravel road about eleven years earlier.

On December 24 the party traveled to Burnt Island by Bombardier 65 miles on the ice. That evening, on a patch of ground cleared of snow, they set up a traditional canvas wall tent complete with wood burning stove. They had noted that there was a good deal of rough ice in the area and that the ice in general was about 2 feet thick. I recall Don McCallum telling me later, somewhat ruefully, that he had spent Christmas day alone at a small fur trading post in Fort Resolution.

On January 1, 1960, they made a trip to Dead Man's Island (Ile Du Mort) for dry fire-wood. During their return they had trouble in rough ice, breaking a sled runner. They abandoned the sleigh about a mile from camp. On January 2, under 20 degrees below F. and a 30 mile wind, they searched on ice for three hours. On January 3 the weather was still cold, 30 below, and the Bombardier wouldn't start. Later in the afternoon when Ashley Pashal, one of the crew, had to leave they took both him and McCallum into Hay River. This effectively marked the end of the inaugural search.

The Captain's Course

Phase Two: April - May, 1960

In late winter, with the lake still solidly frozen in April, Chuck McAvoy, well known bush pilot in Hay River, was hired to fly his plane on searches over the ice. The detector head was mounted on a wing tip and the Amplifier and Esterline Angus Recorder with Harry Hubbard as operator were in the cabin of the plane. Fortunately power could be provided by the aircraft generating system, thereby eliminating the need to carry the heavy 24-volt batteries.

The procedure was to fly courses over the ice at as low an altitude as feasible and, on occasion, to fly parallel courses back and forth at roughly uniform spacings. After quite a few days of random flying with no results someone said, "Why don't we fly the Captain's course?" This is what was done and on April 23, at 3:30 p.m. Harry Hubbard noted "Obtained first Cat signal."

In order to mark the location of a signal a spruce bough was immediately thrown out the window of the plane. The bough was easily found by men on the ice, who marked the location more prominently. The plane then landed and taxied around the location until a maximum strength signal was obtained. A sizeable hole cut through the ice served as entry point for the diver. This time it was Claud McDonald who dove and came

22

up with the great news that a Cat had been found. This Cat was complete with the steel head frame required to lift and lower a bull-dozer blade by cable winch. I recall that in late April Claud came to our office and, with a broad grin, pulled a thin piece of greenish-yellow sheet metal from his pocket. This was a sample taken from the air-filter of the Cat and showed only minor corrosion after nearly 18 years of immersion in the lake.

The Cat location was about 2½ miles north-west of Burnt Island and quite close to the Captain's estimated retreat course from the storm.

Three days later word arrived that the hoisting crew of Willy Arsenault, Fortune LeBouthilier and Guy Tiepel had left Edmonton for Hay River. They arrived there early afternoon the next day only to find that the main road into town was out due to flooding of the Hay River. Someone ferried them out to the lake ice by Bombardier.

In the meantime the plane had kept searching and, surprisingly, Harry obtained three additional good signals in the same general area and these were marked on the ice. He later liked to refer to this as the area of the "3 Cats".

Days of hectic activity followed. Helped by local pilot Willie Laserich and local businessman Sandy Dimion, the men began locating hoisting gear. Some cable, cable blocks, clamps and a pump were obtained from the M.V. LANDA "just in case".

In addition 400 feet of 5/8 inch cable was bought from Ralph Argue Explosives Ltd. for 120 dollars. Fisherman Alex Morin transported this equipment with his "Bug" (Bombardier). Willie stayed to help as diesel mechanic.

The hole marking the Cat was first greatly enlarged by blasting and over this the crew erected a tall timber tripod. Prior to trying a lift, the head frame of the Cat was cut away by underwater torch as it was felt that this would be a major impediment to lifting the machine through the hole. Initially the Cat was left hanging from the tripod at just below water level. Harry had gone back to Hay with Willie to pick up lumber and plastic sheeting for building an enclosure over the Cat. Two Department of Public Works carpenters constructed a plastic tent enclosure in three hours.

Fisherman Harl Broadhead and his "Bug" joined the party on May 1 bringing a propane heater, diesel fuel, transmission and cylinder oil. The Cat was raised that day using the triple blocks with a Bombardier pulling the cable. Timbers were put in place to bridge the hole and the Cat was lowered to rest on these.

Harry recalls that it was a pleasure to work on the Cat because under the May sun the shelter was warm as toast. Work proceeded well and by May 7 the Cat was overhauled and running on the ice. As a reward Willie flew the crew to Resolution to attend a Teachers' Party.

The very next day Harry, Fortune and Guy Tiepel decided to dive at a signal location that seemed the next most promising. Fortune, who did the dive, came up shouting "That's not a Cat, it's a steel boat!" The lake had given up a major secret.

With understandable excitement it was decided that Arsenault, Lazerich and Dimion would use the salvaged Cat to move some equipment to the new site. Willy was approaching near the location when suddenly the Cat broke through the ice and sank. Fortunately the break-through was not instantaneous so that Willy had time to leap off onto "solid" ice. The men had gambled on the spring thaw a bit too long with the result that, unawares to them, the ice had candled, a state under which, although appearing firm, it no longer has the strength to carry heavy loads. The lake was not giving up its secret easily.

This event of course marked the end of this season's search on ice. A couple of days were devoted to clean up loose ends. The equipment borrowed from various government and commercial people in Hay River was returned. Harry flew to Hay River with Willie Lazerich, who then flew right back to Burnt to take compass readings on a few promising locations. This trip, which was to take a day, stretched out to two, making it appear that Willie was overdue. Harry had to keep stalling the Department of Transport from notifying the RCAF and initiating a search. At noon on May 11 Harry left Hay River by car to return to Edmonton.

Phase Three: June, July, August, 1960

Buoyed by their success in finding a Cat and a boat, McCallum proceeded to formalize the group by incorporating a salvage company under the name "Edmonton Search and Salvage Ltd." This name was used for a short time but, to reflect the locale of the work, was soon changed to Northern Search and Salvage Ltd.

A return to the North was scheduled for the end of May. One problem to overcome was an absence of funds. Fortune came to the rescue by borrowing money against his car. The sum of four hundred dollars was received and deposited in the Hay River Bank. On the evening of May 30 Hubbard, Arsenault and Fortune left for Hay River in Mac and Mac's panel truck.

A major salvage operation on water was facing the group and, with low funds, they relied on the good will of various establishments in Hay River. One good contact was a Mr. Landa who owned a fishing business with several good sized boats.

Another was Earle Harcourt who had established a major transportation business in Hay River known as Yellowknife Transportation (Y.T.) which owned several steel barges. Various other deals for borrowing the use of equipment were entered into by Mac and Mac. Landa agreed to let them use one of his boats provided they would first repair it. On June 1 and 2 the crew sanded the surface and caulked the joints. The next day they applied resin and paint to the hull.

Harcourt arrived in town on June 4 and was approached about the use of one of his barges. In the next few days McCallum had discussions with Harcourt about searching for Harcourt's large steel barge that had been lost some time ago by sinking in the vicinity of Hardisty Island. On June 11 Don claimed that Harcourt had agreed to ten thousand dollars for locating the Y-T barge. During this time the Mac and Mac crew who were to do some work on a Harcourt barge were held up for three days because permission was not granted. Negotiations with Harcourt became more complex. He began to put conditions on the salvage of the sunken barge and also wanted a guarantee that nothing further of Y-T's would be salvaged from the lake. This latter was in reference to the SANDY JANE which was a tug owned by Harcourt and named after his daughter. It sank in Great

Slave Lake during a storm; two crewmen were rescued moments before the sinking.

Eventually, much later in April, 1961, a formal agreement was drawn up between Decury Supply Ltd., (a Harcourt company) and Northern Search and Salvage Ltd. in regard to salvage of the sunken barge. A draft copy of this agreement is included here-in as Appendix 2.

On July 2 Hubbard records that a formal contract was drawn up and signed with Messrs Wm. Trefiak and Mickey Kucher for the rental of their barge for a price of 250 dollars. Early morning on July 3 a lifting hoist was positioned on the barge. This was an A-frame made of two inclined steel poles set to overhang the end of the barge, held firm by two cable tie-backs anchored to the barge.

The remainder of July and well into August was occupied by all the activities arising out of a major salvage operation. Just after midnight on July 4 the Landa Motor Vessel CECILIA, towing the barge, departed for Burnt Island. During the trip the barge, being partially filled with water, was emptied of same by an on-board pump by about 7 a.m. when Burnt Island was reached. The CECILIA cast off the tow line and the barge was anchored in the shelter of the east bay.

Harry immediately set up and checked the Magnetometer, then located a suitable landing point on Burnt in anticipation of future landing of the Cat. Willie Lazarich went to get Hector Miron's compass, presumably for flying a proper course towards the Cat location.

On July 6 Harry records arising at 4:15 a.m. His diary for that day has the following entries:

First location 12 noon. Original Cat.

Second location 6:30 p.m. Tug Boat.

In the evening of the next day some further search flights were made, likely to try for locations of the "3 Cats".

On July 8 Harry charged air bottles. That evening, about 7:45 p.m. an unexpected visitor arrived. This was Rudy Steiner, a contractor from Hay River, who flew in together with Alex Arichuck and a Byers Transport manager, landing his Cessna 180 on the east bay. They brought the news that Tom Rimmer was coming to rig up for lifting the Cat. Later that same evening, about 9:30 p.m. the visitors, on taking off to return to Hay River, suffered a reversal of fortune by crashing into the bay. The men were not injured and after being picked up, were delivered to the M.V. LANDA which was at Dawson Landing.

In recent years I have thought of this misadventure as a somewhat ludicrous example of the "Field of Dreams" syndrome: "Build it and they will come." Set up a salvage operation on a sub-arctic lake in Northern Canada and salvage will plunge into your front Bay.

Soon afterward a boat trip was made to Ft. Resolution to wire the British Aircraft Insurance Company requesting authority to salvage Rudy Steiner's aircraft, Cessna 180 India Kilo X-Ray. That evening a check of the bay found the aircraft floats on shore but no sign of the fuselage. I have no record of the eventual disposition of the salvage other than the fact that the Mac and Mac crew pulled Steiner's aircraft engine and cockpit out of the lake and that Willy removed the radios and power supply.

Word was getting around about all the activity. Burnt Island seemed to have become a local stopping point. On July 9 there was a visit from fisherman Harl Broadhead who supplied them with 10 gallons of gas for searching. July 10 was visiting day: The McGuiness Fisheries boat NOR-ALTA was at anchor in the bay, also Northern Transportation Co's RADIUM KING was at anchor with three barges in tow.

On July 12 McCallum, Lakusta and pilot Mel Richmond arrived in a Cessna 180, having been forced down for a day and a half by bad weather en route from Edmonton. Harry flew back to Edmonton with Richmond the next day. At home he received a wire from Willy Arsenault with good news: *"Cat on Burnt Island. Excellent condition.*

Will be running on Thursday night. Weather smooth. Hope to see Harry soon. Regards, Willy."

On July 15 there was a meeting of Ironworkers in a lawyers' office in Edmonton involving Len Clifford, Wm. Abbot, Roy Hicks, Guy Tiepel, McDonald, McCallum and H. Hubbard. The purpose was to draw up a new contract "on disposition of percentages from Cat sales and disposal."

Harry flew back to Burnt with Mel Richmond on July 16, arriving at 8:30 p.m. On checking the Magnetometer he found that it had gone out of calibration on the boys. Afterwards Tracy and Willy discussed methods of raising the boat.

During Harry's absence the boys had borrowed Bobby Porritt's boat in Hay River and used it to carry out a water search in the vicinity of Burnt Island. This was a good quality boat with a Chrysler inboard engine and plastic cabin. Unfortunately a storm came up and drove them onto the rocks along the north shore of Burnt, wrecking the boat. They abandoned it at that location and it remained there for years. As far as I know there was no attempt at restitution.

In the morning of July 18 the water was rough as Harry spent some time in servicing the Cat motor. He had been quite concerned about its condition because the motor had been running when it sank through the ice. He drained oil and water out of the Cat main drive and refilled with oil. Crankcase oil also showed signs of water and needed to be changed. The fuel oil filter had considerable water. Exhaust valves were occasionally sticking on idle. Oil filter screens were sludged up. And, finally, the radiator had several leaks.

By 4 p.m. a general search for more Cats was resumed, laying out a new area with flags. But the water became too rough so the boys dived on the boat instead. They decided it had twin gasoline engines. Local scuttlebutt had it that the boat was transporting army officers and was caught by a following storm with all deck hatches open. Waves breaking across the deck soon caused it to sink.

The next diary entry is on August 12 when Harry recorded that they had re-located the steel "rum runner". On August 13 they began rigging the barge for the lift. The crew consisted of Arsenault, Hubbard, Richmond, Lakusta, McDonald and Le Bouthilier. The lift began the next day. The barge with the A-frame crane was pushed over the boat. The lifting cable was taken down and fastened to the bow-post of the boat. This post was fabricated of two pieces of 4-inch diameter steel pipe assembled in the shape of a Christian Cross. The vertical stem, about two feet tall was welded to the deck and the cross-arm was welded about six inches below the top of the stem. The lifting cable was passed over a pulley at the top of the A-frame and wound onto a winch attached to the deck of the barge.

The lift proceeded smoothly and reached a point where the bow of the boat projected above the water a few feet. At this point the crew was able to make out the name CITY OF NEW ORLEANS painted on the side. The boat was estimated to be about sixty feet long and the water depth forty-five to fifty feet. The intention was to move the boat to Fort Resolution by dragging it along the bottom in this position.

Progress was very slow and travel had only proceeded a short distance when the waves began to build up. The wind increased and it was not long before the boat was being banged against the end of the barge. At this point a decision was taken to release the boat and try again another day. It may have been that the release was actually accidental because the bow-post was torn off the boat and was brought up by the tow cable. It was eventually left on Burnt Island where it could be found for some years thereafter.

Through subsequent correspondence with the National Archives and Records Center, Washington D.C. I was able to learn something about the boat. It was originally named the Motor

Vessel TACONY. Later it was rechristened CITY OF NEW ORLEANS.

Following is a quotation of the pertinent paragraph of a letter dated February 24, 1970, from the National Archives and Record Service, Washington D.C.:

"The only information that could be located was in the files of the Office of the Chief of Engineers on the vessel "TACONY", which is believed to be the same as subject. This information was in the form of a message to the Chief of Engineers requesting that this survey boat be made available to Canol Project for use as a tow boat on Great Slave Lake. No information pertaining to the loss of this vessel was located."

Thus it appears that there is an element of truth in the story circulating locally as to the operation of the boat.

This marked the end of the Mac and Mac searches of 1960. Details of disposal of the Cat are anecdotal. Evidently at first the boys had fun knocking over trees. It is said that the Cat was sold in Hay River for five thousand dollars and that this sum was used up in reimbursing the Ironworkers' out-of-pocket expenses.

Phase Four: Early 1961

Some additional work involving Mac and Mac carried on into 1961. It appears that, following the name change to Northern Search and Salvage, there was a meeting at which Harry Hubbard was elected President. But it seems that Harry was not enthralled by the position. On January 16, 1961, he recorded that he handed over his shares in the Company to lawyer John Kempo and that severed his formal ties with the Company.

However his association with various members carried on. On January 21 there was a meeting between Hicks, Cole and Hubbard. It was decided that Parlee would be the new company lawyer. There was also talk of phoning Johnson in Toronto to terminate the rental agreement on the Magnetometer.

In March of 1961 Harry participated with McDonald in one more search over the ice. In a flight from the east bay of Burnt, after only minutes in the air, Harry received a good strong signal. He retained the print-out of the Esterline Angus recorder. However, for whatever reason, the signal was not followed up.

The roles of McDonald and McCallum at this point were not clear. It is evident, however, that McCallum continued discussions with Harcourt in regard to his sunken barge. These no doubt led to the comprehensive salvage agreement that was drawn up and dated April 27, 1961, but not signed.

My personal contact with both continued sporadically from time to time. The last business contact was when both came to see me about an unusual proposal they had been requested to submit. This was from a dealer in scrap metals who asked for a bid from them for salvaging structural steel from an existing railway bridge. This had been constructed in 1917 part-way across the Nelson River in northern Manitoba but never completed. Too risky for them to tackle, I suggested.

PART FIVE: HUBBARD SEARCH AND SALVAGE
Phase One: The First Search, February 1962

Early in January, 1962, a stranger dropped in at our engineering office. To my surprise he introduced himself as Harry Hubbard whom I had never met. However, Harry and I knew a great deal about each other through our respective associations with Mac and Mac Steeplejack.

I immediately had a good feeling about Harry, likely brought on by his jovial and respectful manner. When speaking with him one would soon be captivated by his unusual mannerism of tilting his head back and, in making a point, roll his eyeballs upwards until only the whites showed, eventually to disappear completely behind closed eyelids. A little chuckle and everything returned to normal.

It wasn't long before the reason for his visit was stated. "You know", he said, "Magnetometers are now being sold commercially by a company in California. The price is three hundred fifty dollars American which seems quite reasonable." The two currencies were approximately at par in those days. Harry carried on "Now in 1961, before we left Burnt Island, McDonald and I did an aerial search from Burnt to the general area north of Pilot Reef and we got a really strong signal." Harry went on to explain that he had kept the print-out record of the signal as well as marking details of the direction, speed and duration of the flight on the signal chart. "I really would like to find that location again. Would you or your firm consider buying a magnetometer and renting it to me for a search?"

Harry's enthusiasm projected great confidence that his data was reliable and that he would be able to relocate the signal again. I must say that I was intrigued by the prospect. The adventures of the Mac and Mac searches were fresh in my mind.

I felt that my partners would not consider the capital cost prohibitive. The truth of the matter was that I really wanted to participate in a search, possible on a part time basis as Harry could use the help. In my mind the time that I would spend would not exceed my normal vacation time of one month per year. In my discussion with my partners I sensed that they saw through my motives. Nevertheless they decided that the firm would buy the magnetometer.

In due course the magnetometer arrived at Customs in Edmonton. It consisted of the detecting head without a brass tube, and an oscillator or amplifier. We turned the amplifier over to Harry to look after.

As a housing for the head, consisting of electrical coils which are the sensors of the magnetic field, I made a protective tube out of

"Sonotube", a hollow cylindrical tube eight inches in diameter made of thick pressed cardboard protected against weather by a waterproof sealant. A pair of internal wooden strips, one along each side, were added to provide support for the brass runners of the head. By adding a sealed fibrous cap fitted onto each end we had our "brass tube". Although not suitable for underwater use it nevertheless would serve quite adequately for searching on a sled, on a boat or on an aircraft wing. Harry rented an Esterline-Angus Recorder and bought two 24-volt wet-cell batteries to complete the magnetometer assembly.

Harry and I decided that we would undertake a limited winter search concentrating on his "west of Burnt" signal. On February 23, 1962, we loaded my station wagon and left for Hay River. The drive on the packed snow surface of the highway was pleasant. On the latter part of the trip, through a forested area, we noticed numerous snow-devils, miniature whirlwinds of blown snow, dancing along the right-of-way.

After an overnight stay in Hay River we awoke to a temperature of forty three degrees below zero Fahrenheit. I then realized that those pretty snow-devils had been harbingers of an arctic cold front moving in. Our car would not start so, while waiting for a boost, we went for breakfast.

The Captain's Course

In the restaurant one of the locals engaged us in conversation. Upon learning that we were about to start a search on the lake he said, "You're too late, John Pope is out there searching right now." Harry knew that John Pope operated a well-respected equipment repair business in Hay River so we simply indicated that we wished him well. Later Harry said to me "Don't worry too much about John Pope's efforts. I'm pretty sure he has a conventional sonar echo-finder. This will locate a Cat provided it beams directly on it, but will also do the same for a large rock on the bottom. It would require a considerable number of set-ups to do a thorough search of even a fairly small area."

After some scouting around we were told that Alex Morin would be the man to see. Alex Morin was a long-time fisherman on the lake, equipped for both winter and summer fishing. Upon locating Alex we found that he had a fish camp set up near Burnt Island and he was going out there the next day. We explained to Alex that we planned to carry out a search for a sunken Cat in the vicinity of Burnt and needed transportation. Alex had a Bombardier, a tracked vehicle for traveling on snow and ice with an enclosed cabin for crew and storage. We told Alex that it would take about a week. He seemed quite interested and offered to take us along on his trip, even inviting us to stay at his camp. Early afternoon the next day we loaded our equipment and bedrolls into the "Bug" and were off to Burnt. It was still very cold but all went well on the trip which took about five hours.

Alex's camp consisted of a wooden caboose on timber skids located about a half mile out in the east bay of Burnt, actually fairly close to where Jones had found the first Cat in 1943.

As we moved into Alex's caboose I made the disconcerting discovery that my best blanket was missing. This blanket had been a wedding present to my wife and I from eastern Canada and was of a quality closely comparable to a Hudson's Bay blanket. On thinking back I realized it had been stolen from my station wagon and I had not missed it in preparing my bedroll to pack in Alex's Bombardier. Later, when explaining the loss to my wife she was not amused.

Late in the evening on the day of our arrival I decided that I should check the accuracy of the magnetic compass of my surveyor's transit. In the year 1962, in the vicinity of Burnt Island, the deviation of the magnetic pole was 32 degrees east of the true North Pole. Therefore I first set the telescope to point in the direction of the compass needle. I next turned the telescope through 32 degrees westward.

Now in the northern hemisphere true north is indicated within a fraction of a degree by the position of the North Star in the heavens.

Therefore I tilted the telescope upwards and was delighted to find that I was looking directly at the North Star. My confidence in the magnetic compass was now complete and I could set the direction of the airplane flight using my magnetic compass if necessary.

The time had come to measure out the location of our proposed search area. To do this we would rely on the print-out of the Esterline Angus record that Harry had retained in 1961, a copy of which is included as Figure 1 following. On the diagram may be seen Harry's annotations as to the location of the signal in terms of direction and distance from the south tip of Burnt.

The next day, starting at the south tip, Harry and I staked out a line on a direction of 83 degrees west of True North (the plane had a Gyro-compass) 12,800 feet in length, somewhat more that the calculated distance of 12,144 feet which would be covered by a plane in one minute and thirty seconds at a ground speed of 92 miles per hour.

Alex came out to our furthermost survey marker in his Bombardier and helped us measure out a one-half square mile area which we felt would cover the area of the signal location.

With the detecting head mounted on a 12-foot long toboggan towed some 50 feet behind the Bug we began our search. But we stopped almost immediately because Harry found that the magnetometer was dead!

There was nothing to do but to check out the electronics of the system. Alex said that he had to go to Resolution so Harry decided that we would take a room at Jim McPherson's Rooming House where we could work with light. After checking a number of tubes Harry found one non functional. Upon checking the socket he uttered the word "Soup!" in some disgust. We then realized that we had set the amplifier in Alex's caboose fairly near the door. Thinking that the crew had probably used the top of the amplifier box as a table during lunch we soon found some soup stains in the ventilation grilles of the box. Using paper napkins Harry was able to clean the offending socket and by mid-night he had the magnetometer working. The next morning was only 25 below but there was a strong wind and Alex said there could be no searching due to poor visibility in blowing snow.

We were beginning to learn about life on the expanses of Great Slave Lake. Excluding the Great Lakes which are shared with the United States, Great Slave, at 11,170 square miles, is the second largest lake entirely in Canada, being exceeded in area only by its neighbor Great Bear at 11,660 square miles some 350 miles to the north. Seen from above, as on a map, many people think Great Slave has the appearance of a

Canada Goose in full flight heading north east, with the neck and head being the east arm of the lake. Generally the lake is a few hundred feet deep but parts of the east arm are two thousand feet deep. Great Slave is far enough south that a viable fishery can be carried on, producing high quality white fish, lake trout, and inconnu, a variation of whitefish. On the other hand, Great Bear is so cold that its fish grow too slowly to permit a commercial fishery. Both lakes are navigable in summer but the safe navigation season in each is rated as the months of June, July, August and September only.

Our stay with the fishermen yielded some new experiences, all seemingly associated with hardship. Pulling out under-ice nets and disentangling fish using wet woolen mitts in 40 below weather was a constant battle with cold. The crew had learned to bury the day's catch in a pile of soft snow as this kept the fish from freezing solid for about 24 hours so they could be transported to arrive unfrozen at the fish plant. Then there was the matter of living in a small caboose on the ice. Although there was an oil heater the floor was always cold. We cooked on a Coleman camp stove. Potatoes, they said, were rendered quite palatable when thrown frozen solid into a pot of boiling water. The men made toast over the open flame of the camp stove by placing bread slices on a inverted tin can with a perforated bottom set to enclose the flame. The result was a perfectly tasty toast speckled with brown spots which I came to call Leopard Toast, and the tin can, a Great Slave Lake Toaster. And I remember one day in early March when the crew said, with evident joy, "The Lake has stopped making ice." To them this measurement from their ice auger was the first sign of the coming spring.

The temperature hovered in the 40 below range and on the coldest day it was 53 degrees below zero in Hay River. Due to the continued cold a major contraction of the ice produced cracks from 2 to 3 feet wide. It was a little un-nerving at night to hear a dull rumbling sound that indicated the cracking and which seemed to be traveling directly toward the caboose. When traveling to search, the Bombardier would occasionally come to a crack too wide for the front skis to bridge across. However the crew had a technique for crossing. The men would jump out and madly shovel chunks of snow into the water until a pile of snow some three feet or more thick was bridging the gap. Alex would then take a run at the improvised crossing and there was always enough buoyancy in the mass of snow to get the Bombardier across.

Harry and I were both pleased to find that we were not bothered whatsoever by the cold. Harry relied on the heaviest Stanfield's combination underwear and I relied on an insulated jacket and trousers underwear combination, newly on the market at that time. And then there were Harry's heat pills, which he said had been specially prescribed for him by his doctor. Every once in a while on a particularly cold day I would hear Harry say "Time for another heat pill!"

We did a few afternoons of searching our designated area and covered the entire half-mile square with passes 50 feet apart. Aside from one or two moderate signals, attributable to bumps of the toboggan, we obtained no valid signals. Thus no Cat was located.

My time for returning to the office arrived all too soon. Harry decided he would stay with the fishermen to search another area. Therefore I set up the transit on our site and we measured another location 6000 feet towards magnetic north for him to search around. At this time we also saw John Pope's caboose in the distance without any signs of activity.

I had made arrangements earlier with Willie Janus who ran a Bombardier freight route from Hay to Resolution. He agreed to pick me up at camp on March 3 on his way back to Hay. That same day Alex told his crew that he would take them to Resolution for a party in the evening. To which news, I remember, the youngest member of the crew responded "Oh boy, piece of tail". I paid

Alex eighty five dollars for gasoline and Janus arrived about 1 p.m.

My ride back with Willie was enjoyable. There was one stop of 30 minutes while Willie waited for the fading of a white-out that was seriously impairing his visibility. When we reached Hay, Willie generously said "No charge" when I enquired about payment for the trip. The temperature had moderated to the freezing point and I was amazed when my car started with a battery that had survived the 53 degree below weather.

I left for Edmonton about 7:30 p.m. and the trip went well for some 250 miles at which point I was flagged down by four native men on the highway. They were lightly dressed and shivering severely in the 25 below night. They asked that I drive them to Keg River Cabins, a small settlement that would involve seven miles of backtracking plus another eight miles off the highway. I objected when I saw they were carrying a gallon jug of wine, but, anticipating my concern, they pointed out that the government seal on the bottle was unbroken. They even promised to pay for the gasoline. On the way I learned that the four men had joined together when two cars, each carrying two of them, had collided head on a mile down the highway. Upon arriving at the Cabins the senior member said thanks and pleasantly surprised me by handing over a dollar bill. Another 60 miles down the highway I reached Manning, Alberta, and a much needed hotel bed.

Phase Two: Harry Alone

After I had left Harry at the lake he was alone until the next day when Alex and the crew returned from Resolution, totally broke. Harry's decision to stay on alone turned out to be a saga of many twists and turns, usually controlled by a shortage of funds. Excepting for one or two trips home to Edmonton, Harry stayed on in the Hay River – Burnt Island area until the end of July.

As soon as Alex returned he asked Harry for fifty dollars, probably to ease his own financial shortage. Later, Alex suggested that he would donate a one-week search if Harry would give him the first Cat found. Harry refused to do this. Harry then went to Hay River where he obtained reasonable accommodation for the following week from Bobby Porritt. Bobby rented him a room above his Hay River Surplus Store at the rate of ten dollars for the week. In the meantime I had sent Harry a cheque for 115 dollars and the office matched that with a cheque in the same amount. I had also sent Harry a sketch map showing him a new area to search based on compass readings taken earlier by Guy Tiepel and Willie Lazarus of

Harry's best Mac and Mac locations. Therefore, I recommended that he move his search to the area indicated on my sketch. Harry wrote back that he had indeed spent two hours with Alex searching the revised area, but without success. Harry also wrote that John Pope had pulled his caboose off the lake on March 14. As far as he knew John had not been successful.

With the arrival of April things began to pick up a little. Willy Janus drove his Bug to carry out a few searches with Harry, all at no charge. Harry then started negotiations with pilot Bob Gilroy for an air search with a Cessna 180 but this search did not go ahead.

Near mid-April, Harry's prospects took a downturn. He entered what he felt was a charter arrangement for a search with another Cessna 180. It resulted in what Harry generously referred to as "the darndest fiasco". The plan started with Harry retaining Harl Broadhead to bring two men from Hay River to Burnt Island with his Bombardier ahead of the airplane flight. The airplane arrived at the island just as the Bombardier was finishing preparation of a landing strip. At this point Harry asked the pilot to fly over the Bombardier at a fairly low altitude to test the magnetometer. After a couple of passes Harry did get a good signal, thereby satisfying himself that the magnetometer was working properly. The plane landed at 4:30

p.m. Right away Harl took Harry ahead so he could finish pacing out the north boundary of his search area. Harry finished quite quickly, then signaled Harl to bring the two men. At this point the starter of the Bombardier failed. Harry walked back to it after which he and Harl walked to the plane which had moved to a closer point. It was then decided that the pilot and Harl would stay to unload the plane while Harry walked about a mile to the island in order to get the other two men. As Harry and the two men were walking back to the plane it suddenly took off, taking Harl Broadhead along. It flew to Resolution, let off Harl, and then took off and flew to Hay River. Harl later said that the pilot had actually suggested that Harl fly back to Hay with him and then take his other Bombardier to go back to Burnt to pick up Harry and the two men. Harl declined because he was under the impression that Willie Janus was actually in Resolution. However, Janus had left so Harl got the Game Warden in Resolution to go out to pick up the men and the disabled Bug.

The Bug's engine started under the tow, but stopped again, so the Warden proceeded with the tow. As they were nearing Resolution the Bug started again so Harry and the men carried on, arriving in Resolution about 12:30 a.m. The next day the pilot wired from Hay at 11 a.m. to see if the men were in. Harry worked a half day rebuilding the starter "from everything but the right parts" as he said. That evening the Bug took them all to Hay River, arriving at 11 o'clock.

Harry couldn't understand why the pilot had acted as he did and wondered if alcohol or lack of it, was involved. He felt that technically as a charter he was abandoned on the lake. Thinking that the Department of Transport would have rulings on such behavior, he asked me to contact the D.O.T. in Edmonton. I did this and was advised that Harry would have to lay a complaint with the Air Transport Board in Ottawa. They doubted that he would have a strong enough case. For a while this experience made Harry feel that there was much to be said for Bombardier searches.

It was May 21 before Harry next wrote me. Things had changed considerably for the better. He had been able to get in 3 hours and 40 minutes of air search using his favorite plane, a Super Helio-Courier, equipped with skis. A new financial backer came forward. It was one of the men on the ice marking straight line courses during the Helio-Courier search. They were after the boat. This time they had no luck but planned another search, weather and ice permitting. Harry said there was another eighteen hundred dollars committed to the search "with no strings attached even if it fails."

The Captain's Course

I spoke with Harry by telephone on May 24 and he told me that Roy Ballsley was the new financial backer. Harry had just come back after taking Roy to the island. Roy showed Harry where Claud McDonald had dropped the boat in August, 1960, as it was being dragged by the barge. Harry said the position is considerably north of the area that they had been searching.

The next chance to search for the boat came on June 2. This time the search was financed by Cecil Rogers, one of Harry's friends in Hay River. Cecil acted as one of the markers on the ice and Roy Ballsley was along in the plane to direct the pilot as to course. Harry picked up some "pretty fair" signals in the area Roy had specified but could not get "right over the boat". In any event there was broken ice and water in the area so no marker trees could be set. Again the search ended in failure but Cecil Rogers seemed well satisfied and told Harry he would be prepared to finance a water search. Cecil was the Sheriff of Hay River and told Harry he was ready to spend the summer on the lake. At that time they were interested in bidding on a department of Fisheries diesel patrol boat that was up for sale but they did not bid. Then they tried to rent a boat but could not find one that was available.

Also about this time Harry and Cecil went to Resolution with Hector Miron, a prominent Hay

River fisherman, to see if Hector's wooden barge in Resolution harbour was salvageable for use by Harry. Nothing came of this.

The idea of obtaining a large boat to serve as a mother ship for servicing motor boats to be used in searching continued to be a high priority in Harry's mind. About this time Harry learned that the Oblate Fathers in Resolution wanted to sell their Mission Boat the Sant' Anna. She was stored on blocks in the Mission boatyard along Sawmill Channel of the Slave Delta near Resolution. When, in late July, a chance came for Harry to fly to Fort Smith, N.W.T. he took advantage of this to see Bishop Piche' about the possibility of buying the boat. The Bishop confirmed the boat was for sale and that the price was four thousand dollars firm. Harry's reaction was this amount seemed "hopeless", so he put it out of his mind for the time being.

Phase Three: The September Search on the Water

Harry's hectic summer, filled with various unsuccessful ventures, was temporarily ended at this point. However, in September Harry and I saw the opportunity to go to the Lake for an autumn search. Harry went ahead in his Morris Minor to arrange for a boat. My wife Pat and I followed a couple of days later. When we arrived Harry told us that Hector Miron would take us searching with his fish boat the Barbara Ann. This craft was a tried and true Lake Winnipeg fish boat with an inboard engine, a Captain's wheel house, a fore-deck housing a large compartment for fish and a smaller rear deck.

Harry and I set about mounting the Detector Head on the bow. While we were doing this Hector busied himself at the stern, installing a conventional flush toilet surrounded by an enclosure of shower curtains draped on a framework of galvanized pipe. My wife and I then realized that this would be the sanitary facility on the Barbara Ann.

After a day's delay due to windy weather we set out from Hay River, at noon, for Burnt Island. We carried Cecil Roger's 14-foot rowboat crosswise on the fore-deck for emergency purposes.

Later that afternoon Harry and I started preparations for a navigation system we had in mind for guiding the boat on parallel courses during a search. Harry had with him about 50 red weather balloons which had been given to him by the weather office in Hay River. Harry, Pat and I began to inflate the balloons which were to serve as line markers on the water. Inflation was by lung power and we were soon blowing them into large spheres about eighteen inches in diameter. These were stored in the fish compartment in the bow. After the compartment was filled we began placing them in Hector's wheelhouse. Before long we had Hector surrounded in a sea of balloons from which, suddenly, a growly voice ordered "Stop, stop, I can't see to steer."

The rest of our plan consisted in using fishermen's net markers that Hector had on board. These were slender poles of black spruce some 8 feet long. A balloon was tied to the top of a pole and a fairly heavy stone was suspended by a piece of thin rope about 10 feet long tied to the lower end of the pole. This was similar to the system fishermen used to mark the location of their nets.

Upon arriving at Burnt Island Hector anchored the Barbara Ann well into the east harbour. Pat and I took the rowboat to shore. The weather was balmy for September so Pat and I set up our tent between willow bushes fairly close to shore. That night the wind came up and we could hear the waves pounding on the shore. Deciding to check the rowboat we found it almost washed off shore. One oar was missing but Pat found it by moonlight a short distance down the shoreline.

The next morning we prepared for a search. Harry thought he had better check the magnetometer. Sure enough, it was dead. The cause was its old nemesis water. We had stored the Amplifier in the fish compartment. The water had come through a hatch cover when Hector swabbed the deck. A thorough drying of a socket with Kleenex solved the problem.

Our search was to be in the same direction as our search of last February but not as far out. To set the direction we first tied a balloon quite high up on each of two trees some distance apart. The line formed by the two balloons was the intended line of search. Hector steered his boat along this line while Harry and I set a row of balloons on the water using the weighted marker poles. We ran the line about a mile and then the boat returned an estimated 50 feet from the line of balloons. There was a light side breeze and after three passes it became apparent that the line of markers became too ragged to provide the hoped for degree of accuracy. We continued a random search for four hours without any signal.

For another two days we searched two areas, one north-west of Burnt and the other between Burnt and Le Roux islands, about three hours in each area. The latter area was a possible location for the American boat "City of New Orleans", however no signal was received in either area.

After these searches the time came to return to Hay River. The return trip was at night and became rather tense when Hector could not see the flashing warning beacon on Mackenzie Rock.

This is a spine of rock that rises above water level fairly close to the usual shipping track between Burnt and Hay. Hector was very uneasy but there was enough moonlight for him to judge his position from the various headlands along the shore which he was able to recognize. All went well and we arrived at Hay River about 1:00 a.m. Hector anchored the Barbara Ann close to the small park adjacent to the mouth of the Hay River. To our surprise Cecil Rogers was there to meet us. Cecil then took Pat and me back to our station wagon.

The next morning we drove back early to the boat so that Pat could cook breakfast for Hector and Harry. Hector seemed mighty pleased to have a breakfast of pancakes and bacon. That ended our trip with the Barbara Ann. As far as I'm aware no one had made use of the outdoor toilet that Hector had so thoughtfully installed.

Harry and Cecil were still not prepared to give up on the lake. They spent over two weeks upgrading Cecil's boat with a new transom, plastic cabin and windshield. The weather stayed warm so that in the third week of October aircraft were still operating on floats. However, windy conditions developed such that Harry and Cecil could not go on the lake that fall.

In November I was surprised to find that, despite my understanding to the contrary, Harry was still President of Northern Search and Salvage. In view of our searching during the summer he wanted to make a final break with the company. At a meeting in November with well known Edmonton lawyer Mr. Parlee, at which I was present, he presented a letter summarizing our activities during the summer, emphasizing that we had not incurred any debts on behalf of Northern Search and Salvage. He then turned over his shares to Tiepel and Cole so they could carry on if they wanted. At the end of the meeting Mr. Parlee took me to one side and, in a low voice, said "You know, I'm not keen on this salvage business, it's just so much Flotsam and Jetsam to me."

Our 1962 search year was over.

Phase Four: The Searches of 1963

The 1963 search year did not begin auspiciously. When Harry left Hay River in the fall of '62 he left the magnetometer at Cecil's place because Harry and I were coming back in the spring. Cecil stored the magnetometer on a bench in his garage.

When spring came, Mother Nature intervened. A sudden break-up of the Hay River in May resulted in the worst flood in the town for many, many years. In Hay River there is the potential for a flood each spring due to a matter of physiography of location. The Hay River rises in

British Columbia well to the south of the lake, flows north through Alberta and part of the North West Territory before discharging into the lake. The river divides into two channels just before reaching the lake. A smaller west channel flows westerly before reaching the lake and the much larger main channel carries on north westerly to reach the lake. The result is that the two channels and the lake create an island called Vale Island. It is on this rather low island that the town is built.

In early May the lake is still frozen with ice four to five feet thick. The river, however, thaws much earlier due to its lengthy inland course to the south. The river ice breaks up and large chunks are carried downstream. The lake ice acts as a barrier and, when the river ice reaches the lake ice a dam of jammed ice builds up very quickly. In 1963 this dam was unusually high, so much so that virtually all of Vale Island was flooded. The flooding was so severe that many boats were washed up and deposited on the main street and various building lots of the town.

Harry made an emergency trip to Hay River to check on the magnetometer, arriving on May 16th. He found that the water had been three quarters up the tubes in the lower amplifier and the leads to the upper oscillator were damp. The two orienting motors in the detector head were full of water and the ball bearings had seized with rust. It took

Harry two days to clean and dry the various parts but in the end thankfully everything was working fine.

Now Harry's attention was directed back to his former item of interest, the Oblate Fathers Mission Boat at Ft. Resolution. Subsequent to his earlier visit to Bishop Piche' the situation had changed. He had succeeded in buying the boat from the Fathers. This was because Harry had sold a quarter section of farmland that he had been given by his father. He sold the quarter for four thousand dollars and apparently convinced Bishop Piche' to accept three thousand as a down payment. Two conditions were that he must pay the balance of one thousand dollars and also remove the boat from the shipyard within one year. In the meantime Harry, without reservation, gave the one thousand dollars to his wife Muriel.

Of course I knew all along that Harry's heart was set on owning this boat. I recall him coming back after his first visit regaling me about the beautiful galley all lined with Vee Groove red fir paneling. She was a sixty ton tunnel river boat of wooden construction, fifty nine point six feet long, designed for pushing barges. She had an Atlas Imperial 120 horsepower diesel engine and was twenty five years old. Harry couldn't get over the convenience of the galley, how it was complete with table and chairs, an oil-fired kitchen stove with a low guardrail to keep pots from sliding off, a refrigerator and a sink. The big diesel engine in a neat engine room, a wheel house with adjoining Captain's Bedroom and an upper deck with a second wheel for fair weather use all combined to capture Harry's heart. She was of course sold on an "as is, where is" basis. She came with a good reputation, having made a number of annual return trips on the Mackenzie River to Aklavic, N.W.T. pushing a barge carrying living quarters for a group of Sisters on missionary work.

A further unwritten caveat was that, in order to operate a boat on public water she must pass a Marine Inspection as to sea worthiness. While Harry was in Hay River he got word that the Marine Inspector from the Coast would be in town the next day. At this time Harry was staying with Hughie Semple, the Airport Manager, whose wife and family were away in Edmonton. Hughie, who had his own airplane, kindly flew Harry and the Inspector to Resolution for inspecting the Sant' Anna. On May 20 Harry received the Inspector's typewritten report, a copy of which is appended.

The most significant item in the Inspector's report was the revelation that there was dry rot in various planks of the hull, specifically in the area of the tunnel and on each of the port and starboard sides. Correction of this problem would involve removal and replacement of planking, not a minor task.

Harry did not immediately convey his reaction to the report to me. Instead I received a letter from him in June advising that he and Cecil Rogers had been camped on Burnt Island for the past week, engaged in searching. They had three barrels of gasoline, courtesy of Cecil, and, as Harry wrote, there was no question that the search would continue. Actually, up to that point, they had managed only one day of searching. He did mention that they had gone to the Sant' Anna and taken the battery charger from the engine room for recharging batteries on the island. There was no further word from Harry as to magnetometer signals.

In July opportunity came for me to devote vacation time to searching. Harry and I planned a trip to the lake for the latter part of July. We evolved a plan to do a water search by boat using Walky-Talky radios for directional control. With two such radios and permits to operate them we drove to Hay River in Harry's Morris 1100.

At Hay we found that Cecil's boat would not be available as the RCMP had requested it for patrol. We also found that boat rentals were prohibitive, twenty seven dollars per day for boat and motor. We then decided to pay Hugh Semple to fly to Resolution where we could rent a canoe. Hughie confirmed he could take us the next morning and invited the two of us to his house for a social evening. We spent a pleasant few hours with Hugh and his wife sharing a few drinks of gin and telling stories. Most of the conversation centered around planes and bush flying. As the evening progressed it was firmly decided that, for normal trapper flights involving one passenger, it would be difficult to overload a plane because baggage would be bulky but relatively light, such as sleeping and duffel bags, tent, snow shoes and a few traps. Nevertheless we told Hugh that we would require two trips to Resolution because of all our equipment plus a couple of cases of beer that Jim McPherson had requested us to bring. By midnight Harry and I had returned to our camp in the little park alongside where the Hay River enters the lake. Hugh was to come at 6:30 a.m. with his station wagon to transport our goods to the airport.

Harry and I rose at 4:30 a.m. and had assembled our gear to go by 6:00 a.m. We had divided our goods by eye into what looked to be two piles of equal weight. Harry was to go first with the magnetometer and I would go on the second trip bringing the tent. Hugh arrived on schedule and took Harry and his load to the airport.

Just after 8:30 a.m. Hugh returned to pick me up. The flight to and from Resolution was fairly lengthy because, with wheel landing gear, Hugh was required to fly over land around the outside curve of Resolution Bay. I had packed everything in good order excepting Harry's Coleman Camp stove which I left standing on top of the iron cook stove belonging to the Park.

The cook stove, being firmly anchored to the concrete floor of what had been a log picnic shelter, was the sole survivor of the flood. It had firmly deflected the large chunks of ice that had neatly bulldozed the picnic shelter off the site. As the stove had been fairly close to our tent Harry had used it as a table on which to set his Coleman stove.

As Hughie and I loaded his station wagon it appeared that perhaps more than half of the goods had been left for the second trip. When we were nearly finished Hugh somewhat nervously asked "Is that everything?" "Almost, I said, except for that little stove over there," pointing at the Coleman camp stove. For a moment I noticed Hugh's upper lip twitching as a look of alarm came over his face. "Does it come apart?" he stammered. I suddenly realized that he had looked at the monster cook stove and had not noticed the Coleman stove on top. I have always felt proud that I did not laugh in his face: instead I calmly said "No, not that stove, just the little one standing on it." Bearing in mind our conversations of the previous evening it appeared that Hugh was not quite ready to give up on the iron monster. When I told Harry about this incident he burst out laughing and, in future, whenever we ran into some difficult problem we would say "Does it come apart?" and then burst out into spasms of laughter. We thanked Hugh for his efforts in getting us to Resolution and paid his charges which we found most reasonable.

At Resolution we were able to rent McPherson's twenty two foot Chestnut freight canoe inclusive of the outboard motor plus a standby motor, all for seven dollars fifty cents per day. Next morning, after loading, a light rain began falling, so instead of going to Burnt we went to the Sant' Anna instead. This proved to be a good move as two days of rain plus a further two days of strong winds meant sheltering in the Sant' Anna. She proved to be a perfect refuge for waiting out the weather.

The Sant' Anna was set up on wood blocks about eighty feet away from the north shore of Sawmill Channel, the most southerly of the many channels forming the delta of the Slave River. She sat about two feet above ground that sloped gently up from the stream, thus she was about eight or nine feet above water levels. She was on property owned by the Mission which it had developed as a boatyard and sawmill area.

During our lay-over Harry and I took time to study the boat. She was obviously well built and, for the time being, ignoring the deficiencies outlined by the Marine Inspector, seemed ready to go. The rotted planks were, of course, a serious problem. The entire hull was formed of 1 5/8 - inch thick Douglas fir planks fastened to interior timber cross-ribs. About sixteen of the planks were weakened to various degrees by what is usually referred to as dry rot. This is caused by an air-borne fungus that attacks wood under conditions of high humidity with warm temperatures. Although the wood is really very damp the fungus consumes the cellulose in the cells, leaving the wood dry and brittle, devoid of strength. In the case of the Sant' Anna the dry rot would likely have developed whenever she was moored on water for a lengthy time during periods of very warm summer temperatures. The most severely affected planks were in the tunnel. This is where the underside of the hull is warped upwards to surround the propeller. The propeller is set so that its lower limits are completely above the bottom of the boat. This feature on river boats is to protect the propeller against damage caused by striking floating or submerged logs.

The Captain's Course

As soon as conditions permitted we left for Burnt Island. It was about a half mile run down the channel to reach Nagle and Resolution Bays. From there it was a straight run of fourteen miles to Burnt. We set up our tent close to shore on the east bay to catch any breeze that might blow away the mosquitoes.

We set our search plan into action by exploring the north shore of Burnt. Here we found an abandoned wooden tower which had at one time supported a navigation beacon for the outer shipping lane. I set up the surveyor's transit on the existing platform located part way up the tower "handy as a pocket in a shirt" as Harry would say. From this platform we had a clear view of our proposed search area.

After some experimentation we developed the following method: Harry would run the canoe on straight line courses away from the island along which I would direct him by using the telescope of the transit. We communicated by calls on the Walky-Talky radios. These worked well except, while the outboard motor was running; Harry could not hear my voice so I had to resort to loud signals from a referee's whistle to keep Harry on course. Harry started a course about a mile from shore, went out for another mile, then turned around to come back along a new course which I would give him using the transit. By turning the transit through a half degree of arc I would set a course for Harry that was nearly parallel to the outward run and about fifty feet over. This was about as close as we could come to the ideal spacing of 50 feet.

After two sessions of four hours each we had searched an area of water about one mile long and varying in width from eleven hundred feet at the far end to five hundred fifty feet at the near end. We concluded, however, that the method was slow and subject to inaccuracies so we abandoned the idea.

We carried out one more search around Pilot Reef and, in cruising around, could see the top of the reef about two feet below the surface. Harry felt he had once received a signal when flying the vicinity of the reef but we obtained no sign of one.

We returned to Resolution on a beautiful calm day, traveling one hour and ten minutes from Burnt. We paid McPherson and stored the magnetometer in his warehouse. As no rides back to Hay River showed up McPherson let us stay overnight in his storeroom. The next day Hugh Semple stopped in Resolution on his way back to Hay. As he was traveling empty he kindly offered to take us back to Hay. This time we sent our baggage home to Edmonton by air freight out of Resolution. At Hay River we sent our two toboggans home by truck freight and then drove back to Edmonton. This marked the end of our 1963 search year.

Phase Five: 1964

The only search of this year was carried out by Harry and his two eldest sons Rob and Neale. For the first time they used Dawson Landing, located near the tip of Dawson Point, as the base for their operations. Dawson Landing, which is six miles by water from Burnt Island, became accessible by auto upon completion of a bush trail from the Pine Point Lead and Zinc Mine. Later a picnic shelter would be built at the Landing by the Territories Government. Harry and the boys searched with McPherson's freight canoe and camped at Burnt Island so as to be more central.

They decided on a number of searches in the vicinity of each Green and Laity Islands. In order to give themselves a reference point as to location they set up a prominent marker on each island. Each marker consisted of a thirty foot long black spruce pole reaching "dizzying heights" by being lashed to the upper part of a tall spruce tree and bearing a cross-arm near its top with shiny tin cans dangling for better visibility. Wind conditions were favourable so they were able to search for several days. The area around Laity would be favourable for a signal from the steel boat but "no luck".

During this trip Harry was able to take Ben Norgstrom, a boat builder employed by Menzies Fisheries located at Dawson Landing, to examine the Sant' Anna. Ben gave Harry a labour quotation of two hundred twenty five dollars for replacing the rotted planks so as to satisfy the Marine Inspector. He advised Harry to obtain Yellow Cedar planks for replacement material because this wood, by virtue of its resin content, was immune to the fungus that causes dry rot.

After carrying out what were called a number of scatter searches Harry sent a letter to Muriel asking her to fly to Resolution and join him and the boys for a holiday on Burnt Island. Unfortunately the letter arrived too late for her to book a flight that would allow her to leave home at this particular time. In view of this Harry and the boys ended this search venture.

Phase Six: 1965 & 1966, Trials and Tribulations

There followed a two-year period when Harry and I devoted a number of trips to the lake to try to develop a more efficient search operation.

In March, 1965, for the first time we were able to drive to Resolution by auto using a newly bull-dozed winter road through the muskeg along the south-eastern perimeter of Resolution Bay. We picked up the magnetometer from McPherson who had stored it for Harry in 1964.

In early May, 1965, we visited the lake to try a new method of travel on the ice. That winter I had observed a winterized off-the-road motorcycle being demonstrated during Edmonton's Mukluk Mardigras winter Festival. With its broad knobbly tires this machine was able to travel through loose snow up to ten inches deep carrying one passenger. I felt it would be worth trying on the lake for laying out search areas more quickly. Upon contacting the distributors' representative I was surprised to find that he was prepared to rent the motorcycle to me on a two week trial basis for the reasonable sum of seventy dollars.

We arrived in Hay River on May 2, just in time to observe the break up of the river. The locals advised that the lake ice would be safe for another two weeks. With the help of a rental truck with driver, facilitated by Joe Scarborough, an engineering acquaintance with the Pine Point Lead and Zinc mine, we were deposited at Dawson Landing on the late afternoon of May 3. There were small pools of water on the ice near shore but further out the ice was bare of snow and still further out there were what appeared to be ponds of water on the ice.

The next morning, when we tried to travel from Dawson Landing across the ice to Burnt Island, we came in for a rude surprise. The ice, although firm, was dimpled with hundreds of bowl shaped depressions similar to large wash basins. They appeared innocuous until we tried to run the motorcycle. As soon as a tire hit a depression the motorcycle tilted sideways and tipped. We could not avoid them. I decided to scout ahead, walking towards Beaulieu Island. On looking back from a distance I saw Harry in silhouette rolling on the ice and the motorcycle sliding on its side. So much for riding the motorcycle. A bit further out I reached ponded water lying on the ice and soon this threatened to top my rubber boots.

Upon rejoining Harry we decided that our motorcycle experiment was a failure. Later, upon discussing the matter with Hugh Semple, Harry realized that we had arrived at the lake just prior to when the ice "raised". Each spring, as melt waters enter the lake, the ice eventually breaks free from shore and rises as it floats freely. It then sheds all snow-melt water wherever it has accumulated. After that time the ice, some 4 to 5 feet thick can be traveled upon for a few days. Nevertheless we decided to send the motorcycle, magnetometer, batteries and Onan Generator back to Edmonton by truck freight, terminating this effort as a search.

What this trip had made perfectly clear was that there was only one conveyance suitable for us during winter searching and that was the snowmobile.

Early in January, 1966, I bought a Skidoo snowmobile together with a trailer to carry it and a sturdy sled with steel runners to be pulled by the Skidoo.

Harry and I made a trip to Resolution in late January to try out our equipment. At thirty five degrees below zero I drove the Skidoo on a test run on the ice to Round Island about two miles out from Resolution Harbour. I was surprised to find that the snow was drifted into low ridges like waves on water but spaced more closely and packed to a rock-like hardness. This made for a rough pounding ride which, when taken somewhat slowly, was quite tolerable.

The next morning we decided to return home. At first the car wouldn't start because of a cold battery. Now Jim and Florence McPherson rarely arose before noon. With great care we partially immersed the car battery in hot water in Florence's kitchen sink. After forty minutes we carefully cleaned the sink and, on replacing the battery in the car the engine started immediately.

When we came to the Dawson Landing turn-off we decided to test the skidoo further by going to Burnt Island. The side road to the landing had not been plowed and was heavily drifted. The skidoo easily handled the drifts and on the lake we found firm snow reasonably smooth. We reached Burnt in under an hour and carried on to our previous search area. Here we found rough ice but, traveling slowly, found enough snow to enable the skidoo to pass through. We arrived back at Burnt after sunset. We were surprised to see the flashing of the navigation beacon on Burnt. This confirmed, as we had previously heard, that the batteries of these navigation beacons often lasted through the winter. We returned to the Landing and our car using the lights of the skidoo, feeling well satisfied with our reconnaissance. That night we stopped in Hay River at the home of Harry's friends Ken and Peggy Hunt.

During our return trip to Edmonton I had time to mull over advantages opened up by the skidoo. I thought, why not build a lightweight caboose on skids and pull it out to Burnt Island to serve as a camp for winter searching?

By mid-March I had built a light weight caboose seven feet wide, fourteen feet long and seven feet high with an insulated wooden floor mounted on two broad aluminum skids. These were donated to me by the metals firm of Westeel-Rosco in Edmonton on the strength of a white lie that I was building an ice-fishing shelter. Walls and roof were made of insulated panels three feet six inches wide by seven feet long, designed to fit within and on top of my station wagon and to be assembled on site using eye bolts through pre-drilled holes in two by three wood studs. We used wing nuts to fasten the through bolts. The floor platform, seven feet wide by fourteen feet long, was designed to fit upside-down on the skidoo trailer so that it would carry the skidoo set between the aluminum runners. Harry provided an oil burning stove for heat. I set up the caboose in our back yard in Edmonton so as to try it out for warmth and ventilation. All wall and roof panels were simply bolted together with no special attempt at sealing the joints. I noted that the structure was quite leaky as to air infiltration and exhaust, assuring a fresh air supply to the stove as well as dissipation of fumes. With the stove set at a normal setting the caboose proved to be a little too warm for the use of a sleeping bag.

I now felt that it was time to set up the caboose on Burnt Island. On March 19 we spent the day mounting the caboose floor on the skidoo trailer and loading all the building panels inside the station wagon and on its roof. The skidoo and stove were fastened on the inverted floor.

The trip north went well until we reached Paddle Prairie, a small farming settlement about half way to Hay River. At a curve in the road Harry, who was driving, noticed that the trailer was swaying. Upon stopping we found one trailer tire flat and its tube ruined. I had forgotten to bring a spare trailer tire! Considering our isolated location Harry mused "It will take a small miracle to get us out of here in less than three days!" Well, the small miracle presented itself in less than thirty minutes. Where we had stopped was next to small grocery store and post office along the highway. We went into the store and mentioned our problem to the proprietor. This was overheard by one of the locals who was in for his mail. This customer said that he had an eight inch wheelbarrow tire with a tube that would likely fit our trailer tire. It turned out to be slightly undersize but, when inflated, expanded to make the tire firm. We promised Don Fleming that on our return we would bring him a replacement tube. We found the proper tube at our next stop, High Level.

Upon arriving at the turn-off to Dawson Landing we again found the road unplowed. We unloaded the skidoo and floor platform and Harry hooked the platform behind the skidoo for a trial run. He soon found that the platform, with its angular corners was becoming jammed in the snowdrifts. We turned everything around, went back to the car, and had lunch. After that I took the skidoo by itself and drove down to Dawson Landing and back, smoothing out the drifts along each side to make a wide roadway. Loading all the building panels on the platform we set off again, finding the load came along nicely. We arrived at the landing about 6:00 p.m., returned to the car and made one more trip to the landing pulling the sled loaded with the stove and other equipment. We then returned to Hay River and spent the night at Ken Hunt's.

The next day everything went smoothly. It took two trips from the Landing to Burnt Island to transfer everything. We were delighted that the caboose platform with its load pulled easily on the lake. We pulled the platform a short distance into the trees from the shore of Burnt's east anchorage. By 9:30 p.m. we had the caboose assembled and the heater working. A very comfortable night was a pleasant sequel to a busy day.

We spent the next two days laying out a search area consisting of squares six hundred feet to the side with corners marked by four feet long pieces of surveyor's lath. This was time consuming and we soon had second thoughts realizing that our scheme would be of little use in an air search. Therefore we packed up our things including the stove, ready for going home. Before leaving we tied down the caboose against the wind. At Hay River we left the skidoo, trailer and stove in Ken Hunt's garage, then headed home. On the way we stopped at Don Fleming's place and handed him his replacement tube for his wheelbarrow, thanking him for his help.

One month later, on April 19, 1966, I left for the lake to join Harry for an air search. Harry had gone ahead a day earlier and I met him at High Level airport just after he had come back from a trial flight with pilot Noel Roger. Harry then told me that he had arranged with Hay River pilot Dunc Grant to fly out of Hay River for an air search planned for the next few days.

This time we were going to carry out a search with four men on the ice to serve as markers for the airplane. Each man would be provided with an eight feet high tripod made of three one by two inch lumber boards over which a black plastic sheet had been stapled to simulate a spruce tree.

Three days before the search Harry, Ken's son Jimmy Hunt and I went ahead to the island and laid out four parallel lines, each one thousand feet long, at right angles to a long base line spaced at two thousand feet along that line. Each man with tripod would start at the base line at each cross line and then move fifty feet up the cross line after each pass of the airplane over him. Thus the total search area would be a rectangle six thousand feet by one thousand feet.

The couple of days that Jimmy Hunt stayed with Harry and I at the caboose were memorable in that he enjoyed himself so much. We gave him free run of the skidoo and did he ever take advantage of it. In certain open areas of the spruce forest there were tremendous drifts of snow over which he created a winding skidoo trail through the trees that he followed over and over again. The snow on the island was so clean that, when melted, there were essentially no particles in the water. Considering other sports such as snow shoeing and cross country skiing I came to the conclusion that winter in the Territories was to winter in Alberta as summer in Hawaii is to summer in Alberta.

On the day of the search two local men, Henry Norn and Henry Sibbeston, Jimmy Hunt and I drove to Dawson Landing and, using the skidoo and sled, arrived at the search area at 12:00 noon which was the time that Harry and the search plane were to arrive. We stationed ourselves one at each cross line, the two Henrys, then Jimmy Hunt, then myself, each with a black plastic tripod.

The plane did not show!

We finally left the site at 4:30 p.m., arriving at Hay River airport at 7:00 p.m. We found Harry there in a distraught state. Dunc Grant would not fly because the airplane was overloaded. Of course, as pilot, he had a perfect right to do this. What had upset Harry was that he had no way of contacting us out on the ice. No physical harm was done. I paid our helpers the agreed fee for the day. However we were unable to arrange for another airplane. Harry asked if I would drive to Edmonton to try to arrange for a plane with a charter company that he knew there. I did so but was unable to come to any arrangement. Harry then drove home in his own car.

Another month later, on May 20, I received a phone call from Harry in Hay River asking me to come up for the weekend. He had arranged for a plane there with Perry Linton, a Hay River contractor with his own plane. I was reluctant to go because of the late date for the ice, but agreed to come. I took Harry's son Neale and my son Walter along and drove through the night arriving at Ken Hunt's house at 3:30 a.m. Leaving the boys sleeping in the station wagon I found Ken and Harry waiting for me in Ken's living room. Harry indicated there was some doubt about the ice and I had a sleep until 6:00 a.m.

I picked up Henry Norn at 8:30 a.m., then Henry, Neale, Walter and I drove ahead for a rendezvous with Harry and Perry at the Pine Point airstrip. They first flew to Burnt, then decided the ice was too soft for landing so met us at the airstrip. This brought an end to our searching for this spring and, as it turned out, the end for the year.

Phase Seven: 1967, The Big Search

Early in the year we took some measures to improve our search capabilities. The first of these was to bring Paul Steffanson, a friend of Harry's, into the search team. Paul was acquainted with Harry through their association as salesmen for a mutual fund. He had a skidoo which he was prepared to bring along on searches.

Next, we bought a five hundred feet long piece of one-quarter inch polypropylene rope which would greatly facilitate the measuring out of a search area. With our caboose on the island we decided we would enlist our sons to help us on the ice. This raised the worrisome prospect of the chance that someone could become lost during a search in the event of a blizzard coming up. In considering this I recalled the legendary method used on the prairies of following fence lines to find the way home. Therefore I purchased six rolls of farmer's binder twine to be laid on the ice starting at our base camp and leading without a break to the end of our search area. As it turned out each roll contained four thousand feet of twine which would enable us to string out twenty four thousand continuous feet of twine if necessary.

About this time the prospect of reserving a Helio Courier aircraft with pilot for an air search in March became more certain. Therefore, in mid-

February, Harry and I left Edmonton with the objective of laying out a large search area. We arranged to meet Paul Steffanson with his skidoo at Ken Hunt's home. During the drive north, on a rough piece of road with some loose stones, the rear window of my station wagon exploded with a bang. Harry's dog Butch, dozing in the back, launched himself into an arc that ended on Harry's lap in the front seat. He stopped shaking as Harry comforted him. Fortunately for us were able to close the opening with a tarpaulin.

Arriving at Hay River at noon we found Ken in his office. While there we met Ken's friend Art DeLancy who informed us that he had seen our caboose in September, in good shape. Paul was late because of wheel trouble on his skidoo trailer. He phoned us at Ken's home in the evening. In the morning, before leaving for the island, we first went to the Fisheries yard where Paul cut the roof off Ken's abandoned station wagon to serve as a sled for transporting his belongings when crossing the ice. When we reached the access road for Dawson Landing we were unable to start Paul's skidoo. Our efforts were unsuccessful so we returned to a service garage in Hay River. In the morning the trouble was found to be a plugged fuel screen. We returned to the island, arriving about 3:30 p.m. We found the caboose on its side, blown over but only slightly damaged. It was soon righted and a Duo-therm heater, given to us by Ken, soon made it warm.

The first night spent in the caboose proved to be cold. The next morning Paul, harking back to his days on a farm in Saskatchewan, busied himself banking snow against all sides of the caboose. Thereafter nights in the caboose were comfortable.

We spent the next three days laying out our search area. This was a rectangular area sixteen thousand feet long by five thousand feet wide lying to the north-west of Burnt Island and to be connected to it by a continuous length of binder twine from its furthest end to our starting point at the south end of Burnt Island. By this time my skidoo had developed gas line trouble. Paul pulled it back to the Landing on his sled and we packed up and returned to Hay River.

Our trips to and from the search area took us past the entry to the West Bay of Burnt Island. It was on these trips we encountered a physical phenomenon which I am at a loss to explain. This bay is buffeted by every westerly wind. On the bay's south shore, which is quite rocky with boulders, we noticed a scattering of large cone-shaped structures of ice. One of these that I later examined, in company with son Walter and a new helper, John Chobituck, was hollow with an entrance opening on what would have been its lee-ward side. It was roomy enough for Walter and John to sit inside comfortably. I can only speculate that during freeze-up these cones were formed by water spray blown by the wind freezing into ice "tents".

The next day we were in touch with pilot George Hart and his boss John Mallendaine of Courier Air Services out of Edmonton. There now appeared to be a good chance of getting a Helio Courier plane with George Hart as pilot to carry out a search in March. Therefore Harry and I decided to return to Edmonton. At first opportunity we bought spare fuel-line parts for both skidoos.

Then I received a call from John Mallendaine advising that he was somewhat pessimistic about getting a plane ready, however, after some persuasion, he eventually agreed to have a plane ready at the island on Tuesday, March 14. I informed Harry of this and we felt we could count on it.

On March 11 Harry and I prepared to head north. That morning my neighbor gave me a five gallon plastic pail from McGavin Bakeries in which I was to pack lunch. My wife Pat and I filled it with fifty seven sandwiches. Harry brought the boys over and we were packed and ready to go by 3:00 p.m. Our helpers were Harry's son Neale, my son Walter and a new boy John Chobituck. Harry's wife Muriel wanted us to take John along as he had been in some trouble with the law and she felt he would benefit by being with us on our northern adventure.

After staying overnight in the hotel at Manning we reached Hay River in early afternoon. We went to Ken Hunt's home and installed the new fuel line on my Skidoo. Peggy Hunt gave us a fine roast beef and Yorkshire pudding supper. That evening we all bedded down in Ken's living room and kitchen.

The next morning we phoned the Department of Transport and learned that pilot George Hart had filed a flight plan that would bring him into Hay River by evening. He arrived at the airport at 7:30 p.m. where we picked him up. During supper we showed George our plan of the search area and explained the use of the boys with black plastic tripods to give him straight lines to fly by.

All of a sudden things came together for the March 14 start. Paul arrived the next morning about 9:00 a.m. Walter and I then drove to the Dawson Landing turn-off and soon Paul arrived there with Neale and John as well as a barrel of fuel for the airplane. The access road to the Landing was open and we were surprised to find that a picnic shelter had been built at the Landing. Moving our goods took some time so it was 5:00 p.m. before we arrived at the caboose. We found that Harry and George had arrived earlier by plane and had gotten camp in ship shape.

Harry, however, was quite unsettled because he had discovered that the nib of the stylus on the Esterline-Angus recorder had been lost. This was serious because it is through the nib that the ink flows to mark the magnetic signals on the record tape of the Recorder. Since we were scheduled to fly the airplane on the search the next morning we decided to try a piece of pencil graphite in the stylus. A trial run indicated that the graphite produced no mark on the record tape. To keep from canceling the search we decided to go ahead and rely on Harry's undivided attention to note any major irregularity in movement of the stylus indicating a significant signal. As each pass of the airplane would take about three minutes I personally had confidence that Harry's unbroken attention would detect a major signal.

After supper George and Harry flew to Resolution for the night. The rest of us, five in all, bedded down in the caboose. Harry and George arrived the next morning after breakfast. Then all of us except George traveled to the search area, laying down binder twine beginning at the south tip of Burnt and extending to the far end of the search area. By 9:45 a.m. we five markers were all deployed at our positions along the south border line of the search area. Thus the view that would face George in the airplane would be five black tripods in a straight line spaced at four thousand feet between tripods.

Our plan of flights was based on the fact that the Detector Head was mounted at the end of the right wing-tip of the plane, that is, about nineteen feet off centre. We had decided that a flight would comprise two consecutive passes in opposite directions along the line. This would mean that there would be some overlap of the Detector's range, thereby providing better coverage. Upon completion of the two passes each Marker would move fifty feet towards the north, measured by a piece of rope. George would return for a flight down the new line and back.

George arrived at the search area within minutes after all the markers were in position. He and Harry began the first flight at 9:57 a.m. By 12:30 noon twenty three flights had been completed, thus averaging about six minutes and forty seconds per flight which included two turns per flight. At this point we all returned to the caboose for lunch. This was the time for Pat's fifty seven sandwiches to come to the rescue. It was amazing to see the rate at which the level of sandwiches went down in the pail, aided by numerous cups of coffee. A bit of Skidoo trouble slowed us down after lunch. We soon restarted the search and went on to complete flight forty seven by 6:10 p.m. George and Harry returned to Resolution for the night.

The next morning was beautiful. The day was crispy cold, pale azure clear, with a haze of frost crystals in the distance. From there came the call of a raven, its sharp rasp filtered to a bugle note.

The plane soon arrived, searched to the completion of flight one hundred and found nothing although Harry noted a weak signal on each of flights 59 and 61. That evening Neale and John went to Resolution with George.

The next morning, March 17, George and the boys arrived a bit late. Neale was sick with the stomach flu. The rest of us extended the east end of the area by one thousand feet and twenty flights were completed. George raised my hopes when he waggled his wings over me on flight 14. Later, when he next met me, he apologized, realizing what he had intended as a friendly greeting would be interpreted as an indication of a signal. George then had to leave for Fort Smith to pick up more gasoline.

That night, with six of us in the caboose, we had to suspend Neale's hammock diagonally from corner to corner below the ceiling of the caboose. He slept well as did the rest of us.

The next day, March 18, George arrived at 12 noon, whereupon we had lunch. After widening the original search area a bit we flew courses 101 to 135. Not a bit of luck. Paul's skidoo broke down on the way back so I pulled his back to camp with mine.

Next day John came down with the stomach flu. It was a good day for searching; we flew courses 136 to 150, then came in for lunch. Afterwards some of us lengthened the area eastwards a bit while George and Harry flew a few diagonal courses towards Burnt Island. After a few more regular courses George had to leave for Fort Chipewyan. Again no signals were received so we decided that this was the end of the search.

The next morning Walter had the flu. He recovered by noon so we decided to break camp. Paul's Skidoo track had broken but he was able to sew it together with wire. We were able to move all our equipment to the junction between the Landing access road and the main road towards the mine. With good fortune we arrived at the Pine Point mine facilities in time to buy a good supper at the mess hall. Thereafter we reached Hay River about 8:30 p.m.

One certainty of our recent search was our satisfaction in pilot George Hart's excellent performance in flying the Helio Courier plane. He was always on time and Harry and I had a saying that whenever we asked George to fly somewhere he would personally be ready in no more than three minutes. George obviously felt that the Helio Courier was a fine plane. Harry used to say that the Helio Courier was a very safe plane because of its slow stalling speed of something like thirty seven miles per hour. We were saddened only two years later when we read of George's death in a plane crash while he was flying a nighttime mercy mission on January 13, 1969 out of Ft. Chipewyan. In that instance George was not flying a Helio Courier and we could not help feeling that if he had been the outcome might have been better.

Most of the way home to Edmonton Harry and I discussed our failure to find anything despite our recent well-run air search which gave us a great feeling of accomplishment. One reason, we felt, was that we were quite uncertain as to the locations of the last three signals in the area of the "Three Cats" that he had received in 1960. Also we were uncertain as to the location of the boat after MacDonald had dragged it towards Resolution and then dropped it.

A more significant reason occurred to us when we thought about the Captain's Course. What the Captain had shown on his sketch map was that part of his course when he was on a direct heading towards Burnt Island. But to reach that heading he must have reversed the entire barge train, changing from a south-westerly heading to a south-easterly one. Harry felt he would have turned into the west wind to do this so as to meet the waves more head-on. The train would have traced a sweeping curve before straightening out towards Burnt. This would have placed the maximum exposure to the waves in the region that Jones felt was the best region to search, i.e. as his Report states: about Due West (Magnetic) (my word, not Jones') of Paulette Island and six miles from Burnt Island. This was in the region that he could not search in 1943 because it was covered by rough ice.

A short while after we had been back in Edmonton some more positive news arrived from Hay River. Harry called me from home to tell me that I had won the prize for the closest prediction of the date and time of the spring break-up of the ice on the Hay River. I then remembered that I had bought a ticket from Ken Hunt of the Legion Raffle as to that year's going-out of the ice. A 100 dollar return on a five dollar investment. On our next trip back to Hay I gave Ken a bottle of whiskey, the traditional reward for the vendor of the winning ticket.

PART SIX; THE SANT' ANNA
Phase One: Trial Repairs

Despite our disappointments in each of our searches to date, we were by no means ready to give up on the Cats. Harry kept thinking about his idea to use the Sant' Anna as a mother ship to service a small number of motor boats for searching in its vicinity. This would of course entail restoring the Sant' Anna to seaworthiness. Harry had from time to time spoken to experienced boat builders at chance meetings in Hay River and had received advice from them as to procedures required in replacing the rotted planks in the hull. After talking with him about this for some time I became quite interested in the prospect of restoring the Sant' Anna. By this time Harry had purchased the necessary yellow cedar lumber from Clark Lumber in Edmonton, buying their entire supply of this relatively rare lumber in our area. The momentum for carrying out the repairs was increasing; therefore I decided to help Harry. We did not discuss any arrangement for doing the work but just carried on naturally as we had in the past.

In August, 1968, we headed for Resolution to begin work on the boat. We went in separate cars, Harry taking his son Neale and I taking my son Walter. Shortly before reaching Resolution we stopped at Dawson Landing for a lunch break. As there happened to be a native with a motor boat at the Landing Harry and I hired him to take us out to Burnt Island so that we could check on our caboose. Upon our arrival we walked into the bush towards our caboose and stopped in disbelief, **IT WAS GONE!** The caboose had been towed away including all our tie-down ropes.

The remaining distance to Resolution proved difficult because Harry's Morris Minor kept getting stuck in sand dunes through which the bush road led. Extricating the Morris proved quite easy. We passed a long tow rope around the entire body of his car and pulled the Morris through the sand with my station wagon.

At Ft. Resolution we contacted Father Menez who showed us where the lumber that Harry had shipped ahead by truck was stored. We then rented a canoe from Angus Beaulieu and a motor from Jim McPherson. A short trip across Nagle Bay and up the Sawmill Channel brought us to the Sant' Anna.

Here we made a tentative attempt at setting a new plank. First we took out one of the less curved planks that had dry-rot in it. Next we had to improvise a boiler and a steam box. For a boiler we set an empty 45 gallon oil barrel over a hand-dug depression in the ground in which we would build a wood fire. We fashioned a steam box by covering a wood framework approximately 2 feet by 2 feet by 14 feet long with an insulating blanket made of two sheets of polyethylene film between which we placed two-inch batts of fiberglass insulation.

We cut a piece of yellow cedar plank to the same shape as the board which had been removed, then put it in the steam box. Our boiler worked well and produced lots of steam which we piped into the steam box. After two hours we removed the plank and began to set it across the ribs of the boat, holding it in place with carpenter's clamps. Tightening up the clamps showed that the board was still very stiff and highly resistant to bending. Not long later the board broke under pressure. Our steaming had not worked. Our conclusion was that the steam box did not maintain the steam under pressure and not enough moist heat was penetrating the wood.

One further attempt seemed worth trying. This time we decided to boil a piece of plank. This was because I had once used this method with some success in bending a piece of spruce-board. We boiled a short piece of cedar plank in an open 45 gallon drum for four hours, then tried to twist it with large wrenches. It did twist some without breaking but we decided that more boiling would be required and that this did not appear to be a practical method.

Walter and I had to leave for home after a relatively short stay. Harry and Neale stayed a few days longer so as to close up the Sant' Anna for winter.

As it turned out I had just returned to Edmonton when a business call took me to Ft. McMurray on August 14th. Knowing that the Sant' Anna had been built in Ft. McMurray by shipbuilders Denholm and Currie I was delighted to find the name of Russell Denholm in the directory. Russell readily agreed to see me when I called him.

Russell appeared to be about seventy years old and was in excellent physical condition. He said that he had built the Sant' Anna himself in 1938. When I told him about the yellow cedar he recommended that we use edge grain fir for the tunnel boards as it "takes the steam better, will twist more easily and will wear better". He had used a "15 pound" boiler to produce lots of steam although he did not pressurize his steam chest. His chest was made of wood, about sixteen inches square inside and arranged so that the planks were held about two inches above the bottom so they would be surrounded by steam. He used the steam for only forty-five minutes and one end of the chest was simply plugged by gunny sacks.

He said that when we replace planks the centre plank should go in first. He felt that, in general, the caulking need be tightened up only but to do this the white lead must first be raked out. And, as a very practical suggestion he felt that putting a foot of water in the hold would be a good way to "tighten her up".

I came away convinced that a good supply of steam at good pressure was a necessity. Generally I was encouraged by his words. And, in the year when we returned to carry on with the repairs, the matter of a supply of good steam solved itself.

Phase Two: A Major Breakthrough, October, 1969

Harry had gone ahead to the boat in early October, 1969. After attending a business meeting in Northern Alberta I carried on with my station wagon to meet Harry in Resolution on October 16. I had informed Harry that I was bringing a 3 ½ horsepower outboard motor so he had rented a suitable rowboat from Angus Beaulieu. We loaded the rowboat with various items for our work and just before sunset took off to go to the Sant' Anna by water. This involved starting in Resolution Harbour, traveling around Mission Point to reach Nagle Bay, then crossing Nagle Bay to the outlet of Sawmill Channel and then going up the channel about a half mile to reach the boat.

The Sant' Anna was located on a piece of land owned and developed by the Oblate Missionary as their boatyard and sawmill area. It had been surveyed into River Lots in 1923 and, years ago, cleared of native trees and bush into an open work area. By the time of our visits the clearing had been diminished considerably by younger trees moving inwards from the old trees representing the limits of the original clearing. Not far upstream from the Sant' Anna, in the same yard, stood a well built but unfurnished two storey wood house for the use of workers in the shipyard during summer.

Our first repair work was to remove and replace the only two ribs in the boat which had been damaged by the dry rot. These were just astern of the galley and came out easily as soon as we removed the nails which attached the planks to the ribs. We then cut exact duplicates of these ribs from the yellow cedar that Harry had supplied, using a hand held fret saw which had belonged to Harry's father. We then fastened both ribs in their proper positions using lag screws through selected sound planks of the hull.

Harry's early arrival at the site had had unexpected beneficial results in that he was able to thoroughly explore the shipyard. In the growth of young trees next to the old forest Harry discovered a Ferguson Ford Tractor and a high pressure fire-tube steam boiler. Both appeared to be in reasonable working order. It wasn't long before Harry had the tractor repaired and running. He then cut a passage through the young trees and dragged the boiler on its skids with the tractor to a position near the Sant' Anna where he set it up on blocking, ready for use. At Resolution Harry had obtained a piece of large steel pipe, 10 inches in internal diameter, 9 feet long, of three-sixteenths inch thickness. This pipe was open at one end and closed at the other. Harry's plan was to set this pipe upright next to the Sant' Anna with the closed end down, fill it with water and conduct steam into the bottom with a hose and then use this arrangement to boil the new planks.

The weather had turned colder and light snow began falling. We turned our attention to what we called the keel plank. The Sant' Anna didn't have a keel; there was a longitudinal plank along the very bottom centre-line of the boat. This plank, in the position that a keel would normally occupy, gradually curved upwards near the stern to form the topmost part of the propeller tunnel. Part-way up the curve it had a 2 ½ inch diameter hole to permit passage of the 2 ½ inch solid steel shaft from the engine to the propeller. One of the terms of the sale of the boat was the supply of a brand new stainless steel propeller shaft because the original shaft was damaged.

We removed a section of the existing keel plank and prepared a replacement piece of yellow cedar which we had to rip for its entire length of sixteen feet. After temporarily fitting the replacement piece in position we marked where the drive shaft would pass through. Since the shaft passes through the keel plank at an angle we twice practiced cutting a 2 ½ inch hole at the proper angle through a sample board at the same angle. This is not an easy task as, because of the angle, a circular hole appears as an ellipse on the surface. Then, again using Harry's fret saw, we cut the hole in the keel plank. Our completed hole was just slightly under size, meaning that we could ream it to get a perfect fit for the shaft.

Our allotted time at the Sant' Anna was coming to an end so we put things in storage in preparation for leaving. The lumber was put under the floor boards of the engine room. We decided not to lock the Galley. On leaving we went down the channel only to find Nagle Bay frozen. Our exit route was blocked. Our alternative way was taken by Harry who took the motor boat up the Nagle Channel for some considerable distance to reach a sawmill at the junction with the Slave River. I walked to Resolution to pick up my car which the Mounties had stored in their yard as protection against theft. When I informed them of my plan to drive down the bush road to pick up Harry they felt the drive would be difficult. Nevertheless I proceeded, banking on the ground being frozen. I found that the road had been scarred by deep ruts left by a Caterpillar tractor some time before. The only way to proceed was to straddle one rut, keep one wheel on the high ground between the ruts and keep the other wheel on the high ground at the side of the trail. Progress was slow as it took 1 ½ hours to go 8 miles. As I was about to reach the Slave I met Harry coming towards me riding in the Game Warden's truck loaded with the motor boat. Fortunately there was a level area for me to turn around and head back. Harry came with me and we had as extra passenger a four year old native boy who was to return to Resolution. The boy sat between Harry and me and watched every movement that I made in driving. This must have been a new experience to him as, when I glanced down, I saw a look of wonderment in his eyes. A line from Sara Teasdale's poem BARTER sprang to mind:

"And Children's faces lookin up, holding wonder like a cup".

Apart from that this trip was more like a nightmare for me. During most of this latest stay at the Sant' Anna I was plagued by Iritis in my right eye. This was an affliction that seemed to return every five years. With the low October sun and a line of spruce trees on the sunny side of the road I found myself driving between rapidly alternating bright and dark patches of light, a condition to which Iritis is particularly sensitive. There was nothing to do but cope as best I could.

We arrived safely at Resolution. After paying Angus Beaulieu for his boat Harry and I proceeded towards home, stopping at Pine Point for late supper at the mine mess hall. We then drove on with Harry going to Hay River and I turning south towards Edmonton. On the way home the next day I stopped at the hotel in Valleyview as my eye was aching strongly. A good rest following the application of a number of hot compresses to my eye did a world of good and by the next morning the Iritis had subsided.

Phase Three: 1970, Progress by Erratic Steps

In late February, 1970, I was scheduled to visit two locations in Northern Alberta on engineering matters. On mentioning this to Harry he said he would like to return to the Sant' Anna in order to transfer the anchor chain to the boat. My trip evolved to include Harry, the skidoo, trailer and sleigh, extended to include the anchor chain transfer. After calling at the two locations in

Alberta we eventually arrived at Ken Hunt's place late in the evening of February 24. We spent the night sleeping in the station wagon, kept warm by Ken's in-car heater.

The next morning we visited Art Delancy. He told us that our caboose was at Union Island. This is an island far up the east arm of the lake, in Hornby Channel, near the upper end of the Simpson Islands. The RCMP had told us earlier that they had heard rumours that our caboose was on one of the Simpson Islands. I imagine that its aluminum runners will survive in some form to make high class runners for a fisherman's caboose.

The anchor chain was stored in an open 45 gallon gasoline barrel located in Angus Beaulieu's back yard. The chain was four hundred lineal feet of galvanized five-eighth's inch steel links in total weight of close to one thousand pounds. Fortunately it was a mild day close to the melting point because the chain was frozen in snow in the barrel. By the laborious process of "cracking the whip" with the chain itself, after an hour we had removed the entire length from the barrel. We loaded it on the trailer and took it by bush trail to a landing near the lower end of Sawmill Channel where it empties into Nagle Bay. To load it onto our sleigh we had to place it in progressively diminishing coiled layers, resulting in a pyramid shaped pile well over a foot high. The skidoo was just able to pull this load but, due to varying hardness of the snow, the sleigh kept tipping so we abandoned this method. Instead we dragged the chain directly with the skidoo but found that after 300 feet the friction caused the skidoo to spin out. We would then go back to pull from the other end, only to be stopped again after another 300 feet. Eventually we moved the chain close to the estuary of the channel. Leaving the chain I then made a double skidoo trail on the channel ice from the Sant'Anna to the chain. The next morning we went down the channel early. After loading the chain on the sleigh we started pulling it along the double trail that was now firmly frozen. In thirty minutes we accomplished what we had been unable to do the day before. By mid-afternoon, using the capstan, we had the entire chain in the hold of the boat.

Having accomplished the main objective of the trip north we returned to Hay River where we again slept in the station wagon parked in Ken's yard. On the journey home we attempted to contact Ben Norberg, a boat builder in Lesser Slave Lake but were unable to locate him. We arrived home on March 2nd.

In early fall, 1970, Harry Hubbard with his youngest son Colin and my eldest son Walter drove to the Sant' Anna some days ahead of me. I arrived on August 29 and was able to drive almost to the head of Nagle Bay carrying the family canoe on my roof-top carrier. After sleeping in the station wagon I left the car there and paddled across Nagle Bay and then up Sawmill Channel. Harry and Walter were stoking up the boiler when I arrived. They had built a form to match the shape of a substantially twisted plank that they wished to replace. The next day we got steam up and boiled the plank. With the boiler arrangement we were able to feed high pressure steam into the bottom of our boiling tube. As soon as it was released from its pressure chamber the temperature of the steam would revert to just under 212 degrees Fahrenheit. However, as it was in ample supply, it kept the water boiling at close to 212 degrees Fahrenheit. After several hours of boiling we were able to clamp the plank onto the form without much difficulty. We were elated as this represented a real breakthrough. Late that day Ken Hunt and his youngest son Bruce arrived for a visit. That night our visitors and I slept in the empty Mission house.

We now felt we were ready to do a preliminary installation of the keel plank. Because of the limited length of our boiling tube we boiled the plank for about two hours and then turned it end for end in the tube to boil for another two hours.   Using five hydraulic jacks and four carpenters' clamps we were able to bend it to its proper position on a temporary basis. The hole for the propeller shaft was about a half inch too high but this would be corrected by moving the plank down the curve at a later time.

At this point everyone was loaded into the motorboat, and placing some baggage in the canoe, we left for Resolution to see off Harry and Colin who were returning to Edmonton for Neale Hubbard's wedding. The next day Walter and I took out the keel plank, sawed off one and five eighth's inches and set it back in position. The hole for the propeller shaft lined up perfectly. We then permanently fastened it in place using lag screws.

Although the planks of the hull had originally been fastened using standard 5-inch spikes pounded in place by hammer, Harry vowed that he would use only wood screws in the repair work "because you can take them out without wrecking the wood". This required an under-size hole to be pre-bored through the planks and into the ribs for each screw. Then the screws, which were 5/16 by 5 inch lag screws, were turned into the hole by hand ratchet. This method produces a positive fastening with control over the tightness of the fastener. It took almost two days for Walter and I to set the keel plank including another 6 foot piece butt spliced to the original by a scab piece, but we were well satisfied that it was properly in place.

While we were alone Walter slept down below in the crew's quarters and I slept above in the Captain's Cabin. One night I suddenly awoke from a sound sleep to see what appeared to be flames licking at the opposite wall of the cabin. This alarmed me, especially when looking up the flames seemed to be racing across the ceiling of the cabin. Gradually my mind realized that, because there was no heat, perhaps the flames were outside. Upon getting up I could see a flickering light coming through the small window at the head of the bed. Looking out I discovered that two native youths had built a huge bonfire some yards away from the boat and were lying on the ground getting warmed by the fire. I decided that the situation was not dangerous and went back to sleep. The next morning the fire was out and our overnight visitors were gone.

During variable weather of the next week Walter and I decided to tackle an area where the rotted planks were both curved and twisted. This presented the problem of exactly how long a new board must be in order to fill the length of the gap. Earlier Harry had learned from a boat builder that in such a situation one must resort to "spiling". This involved choosing a piece of thin, narrow and flexible board and temporarily clamping it in place to follow the curved and twisted gap. Upon releasing the board one has the necessary centre-line length for the required plank. We successfully used a board about 2 ½ inches wide and 5/16 inch thick. Progress was slow with the result that we put in only one twisty board initially.

During inclement weather we were blessed with a warm dry Galley, thanks to Colin Hubbard's earlier work in fibreglassing its roof. I spent some time picking black currants to go with hot cereal and Walter prepared a couple of tasty meals of oven-roasted rabbit.

One day I started to dig a trench under the Sant' Anna in order to give ourselves standing room in order to make it more comfortable to work in the underside of the hull. Excavation was easy until I hit a hard layer which I thought might be sandstone. However, it was a blue-grey colour that came out in cold pieces. I then realized I had hit permafrost ice. That was the end of the digging. There was an improvement though because, as the boat was up on blocks, we could now just stand erect under the tunnel portion.

Another day we decided to haul more firewood. We chose to tow the canoe behind the motorboat so as to have a vessel for the firewood. We learned an instant lesson in towing a canoe. Not knowing any better we connected the tow rope to the top point of the canoe's bow. The following canoe immediately began to yaw sharply and ship water. We stopped the tow before the chain saw in the canoe fell out. A short time later a native came by towing a canoe with a motorboat moving at a good rate. I noticed that his tow rope came out of the water from under the bow of the canoe. With this arrangement the canoe was lifted slightly at the front with the result that the stern was acting as a rudder. Thereafter we had no trouble towing a canoe.

On September 12 we learned through our radio contact with the Hudson's Bay Manager at Resolution that the Hubbards were back. We finished clamping the plank in place and then went to Resolution to pick up Harry, Rob and Colin. They brought back some news that posed a new problem. Some time ago Harry paid off the remaining thousand dollars that he owed on the Sant' Anna. Now he had the word from Bishop Piche' in Fort Smith that the Mission was anxious to have the boat moved off their sawmill property by October 1, 1970. This would be extremely difficult for us as we would not have the boat repaired in time.

We recalled that someone had once told us that the Mission Property on the channel was Lots 5, 6, 7 and 8. We thought well perhaps we could just move the boat off their property. But where exactly were lots 5 to 8 and where on these lots

was the boat located?   Now all along we knew
there had been a legal survey of the site because
there was a surveyor's pin protruding from the
ground just under the portside hull of the boat.
The pin was capped by a brass medallion but, as
the medallion could be rotated by hand we had
paid little attention to it.   There was a stamped
insignia on the cap as shown.   We did not
understand the meaning of the insignia but
recalled having seen one other pin in the area with

a cap that did not rotate.
We decided to look for more markers in the
vicinity.   After about an hour we had located five
additional pins, widely scattered.   At each of the
other pins we found traces of four square pits that
land surveyors used to dig around a survey pin to
mark the location.   By plotting the relative locations
of all six pins, based on paced measurements, we
could see the property had been surveyed as a
series of adjoining rectangular river lots with the
number 1 designating the north-east corner in
each case and the numbers 2, 3 and 4 being in
counter clockwise order at the other corners of
each lot.   This meant that the pin under the boat
indicated corner 3 of Lot 6 and corner 4 of Lot 7.

Our finished sketch showed that the boat was straddling the line between lots 6 and 7 which happened to be the middle of lots 5, 6, 7 and 8.

In order to be off the Mission property the boat would have to be moved at least five hundred feet. After a brief discussion we decided this would not be feasible. Harry, who knew Bishop Piche', felt we should go to Fort Smith and ask the Bishop for an extension. The next morning Harry, Rob and I drove to Fort Smith. Our reception by the Bishop was most cordial. Harry broached the matter of extending the deadline for moving the boat and suggested we would have the boat off by July 1, 1971. Evidently Harry had paid by certified cheque which the Bishop still held. There was a brief discussion that the fog bell was missing from the boat and the Bishop felt that they still had it. The agreement was that the Hubbards would advise their lawyer that the certified cheque could be released without the fog bell being turned over immediately and the Mission would provide the bell sometime before July 1, 1971. We were much relieved and arrived back in Resolution about 9:00 p.m.

The return to the Sant' Anna by motorboat after dark wasn't without incident. After having coffee with Grant Scott, the Bay manager, we started out on Nagle Bay towards the Sant' Anna at 10:00 p.m., facing a strong head wind. We were fortunate to find the channel markers right on and then suddenly hit a dead-head. This broke the shear pin of our outboard so we paddled into the channel. Soon we met Walter coming down the channel by canoe with the lantern as Grant had advised him by radio of our departure.

The next day we put the remaining lag screws into the twisty plank. Then Harry and I spiled the next long twisted board. I plotted a diagram of same to show Rob how to determine the width of plank required to allow cutting out the curved board.

It was then time for me to load up the canoe. Walter towed me to the landing by motorboat. After loading the canoe on the station wagon I traveled to Peace River and arrived in time to carry out an inspection of the Peace River Television Tower.

Phase Four: The Launching of the Sant' Anna

Faced with prospect of making the boat seaworthy by July 1, the Hubbard family and Walter and myself were determined to start as early as possible. We planned to start May 1 but car trouble and pressure of business delayed my departure until May 7. However Harry, Rob and my son Walter went ahead on May 3, departing at mid-night.

In the meantime the Hubbard family were busy preparing stockpiles of food for a lengthy stay at the Sant' Anna. Led by Harry's wife Muriel, Rob's wife Elizabeth and Elizabeth's mother Mrs. Burch, they organized a 12 day rotation of menus of luncheon meals, all packed in boxes in a scheduled order as would be suitable for a mountaineering expedition. All of this was loaded into my car and trailer, also in Neale's car, after which Neale, Colin and I left in separate vehicles late on May 7.

The next day we ran into a heavy snowstorm in far northern Alberta. It eased off a bit and then strengthened just north of the Territories border, bringing 6 inches of snow. I had coffee at the Hunt's, then left for Resolution, arriving at mid-night. Harry was there with a place for us to sleep at McPherson's.

On May 9 we drove to Nagle Landing at the channel a mile or so upstream from the Sant' Anna. Here we unloaded all the boxes of food for transshipment to the Sant' Anna by canoe. In the vicinity of this landing we discovered some old abandoned stockpiles of cordwood logs in the bush. Soon thereafter, with all the help at hand we loaded the canoe with 4 ft logs and floated the load to the Sant' Anna to provide firewood for the boiler. I then had to return to Edmonton while the rest of the crew stayed to carry on with the repairs.

At Edmonton I had a special mission to carry out for Harry. He asked me to buy five gallons of sheep's tallow to fill the stuffing box in the Sant' Anna. This would serve as the watertight seal in the bilge where the propeller shaft enters the boat through the hole in the keel plank. It had been recommended to Harry that sheep tallow was the best to use. The action is the rapidly spinning shaft soon melts the tallow through which it passes, stopping any water that tries to enter alongside the shaft. My local Safeway store was enlisted to find sheep tallow for me, however they found that local rendering plants had stopped saving sheep tallow some years ago. The result was that I settled for beef tallow which the store sold me in a five gallon pail for ten dollars. I hoped it would work.

I arrived back at Resolution on June 19 about 8 p.m. I asked Jim Cameron, the new Bay manager, to call the Sant' Anna for me but there was no answer. I was about to leave for the channel when Colin and Walter drove up – it turned out that they could hear us but we could not hear their reply.

There was a major change in the Sant' Anna. Nearly all of the planks were in place and she was up on rollers ready for launching. The speed-up in replacement of planks could be credited almost entirely to Rob Hubbard who had developed mastery in boiling and fitting the bent planks. This aspect of the work was most satisfying.

The usual way of launching the boat was to sent her down a greased inclined slipway of 12 x 12 timbers. There were a number of 10 x 12 and 12 x 12 timbers on site from previous launchings but we would require more. At any rate, Harry did not favour a slipway. Instead he built four substantial timber cradles of sawn lumber to support the weight of the boat. By means of hydraulic jacks he lifted the cradles bearing the Sant' Anna onto a number of large tree stems to serve as rollers once we decided to move the boat down to water.

The new driveshaft and its steady bearing in the tunnel had not yet been installed. The next day we spent considerable time in smoothing out the earth along the launching path. Also there was a sharp drop of about a foot at the water's edge which we evened out to merge with the slope of the launching. After lunch we had a visit from the Hunt family: Ken, Peggy and their younger children Bruce and Barbara. They brought roast beef for supper which was most appreciated.

On June 21, the longest day, we moved the boat two feet towards the channel using Harry's manual "monkey winch" which provided a multiplication factor of fifty, plus some jacks loaned by the RCMP. Harry started installing the propeller shaft but ran into trouble aligning it with the engine. He was sure this was due to the boat being somewhat distorted by the moving. Our attention was diverted as we all had a laugh when Walter, who had laid his gloves on the ground, found a bunny rabbit fast asleep in one of them when he came to pick them up. It was just a baby so he set it back in the bush.

Finishing touches for launching continued for a day or two. Some of the bolts for the steady bearing were missing but Harry found some in Resolution. The steady bearing is the first support for the propeller shaft just before the point of attachment of the propeller. It is a triangular arrangement of steel braces attached to the underside of the tunnel by means of lag screws through the planks and into one of the ribs. Colin and Walter put in the last two butt splices and caulked the last seams.

In removing planks from the hull we were able to observe the manner in which lateral contact between planks had been caulked. The edges of the plank were beveled slightly so that a narrow vee-groove existed between planks beginning about three quarters of an inch outwards from the ribs. A strong cotton string was the first item forced into the groove. This was covered by a firm paste which we called white lead. Following the white lead, oakum caulking was forced into the groove to end up flush with the exterior of the hull.

About this time Harry came to me saying he would like to give me a share in the boat to compensate for the time and expenses that I had devoted to helping him. He suggested a fifteen percent share. I thought this would be ample and felt honoured. However, in discussing this with Walter, I realized that I really did not want to get involved in the operation of the boat. All along I had looked on the boat as a Hubbard family project and for me she was only an engineering challenge in her rehabilitation to a working vessel. I did not pursue the matter with Harry and we carried on in our usual manner.

On June 23 the boat was moved ten feet closer to the water. The twelve day menu was proving popular and occasionally inspiring. Today was day seven of twelve. On June 24 we were able to incorporate newly found timbers into the launch way, thereby smoothing out the slope.

A message arrived from Resolution requesting me to phone my office. My partners asked that I fly down for a few days to attend a meeting about a new design project. I flew to Edmonton the next day. While at the Hay River airport waiting for the plane I had a chat with Hugh Semple and Don Barker, his assistant manager. Don informed me that Rudy Steiner and John Pope claimed to have found the Cats and the Boat, i.e., everything, with their magnetometer. I made a mental note that this information was "too good to be true".

I returned to the Sant' Anna on Thursday, July 1. The boat stood at twelve feet from the water. The propeller shaft and steady bearing were in place and the propeller turned smoothly. The channel water was quite muddy so the boys imported two gallons of drinking water from Resolution.

Friday was a productive day with eight large timbers set in final position. About 5 p.m. we began jacking her down the ways and by 9 p.m. her port side was at the water's edge. We decided to start the launch in the morning, July 3. Our first act that morning was to melt the beef tallow which we did in a small barrel over an open fire. When poured into the stuffing box with the driveshaft in place, the tallow filled the box flush with the top.

We started by using one jack to push the bow towards the channel and bring the boat more parallel to the current. Walter held back the stern with the monkey winch, gradually releasing this so that the stern could follow the bow. Soon she began to go by herself. Colin and I held back on the bow but our anchorage slipped and suddenly the bow swept forward into the water. The stern stayed on land. The bow began to take on water quickly. We installed a pump and this began to help. I found myself worn out; evidently the sardine sandwich of that day's luncheon menu had been used up. I retired to the mission house for a short nap. During this period Harry fastened the anchor chain to the bow post. When I returned he was about to fasten this to a deadman when suddenly there was a snap of breaking timber, the boat sighed a bit and the stern slid down the ways into the water. Harry's comment was "Pretty nice, eh". She swung broadside to the stream and hung there. Colin and I pulled her bow in towards shore. She still had her cradle timbers under her. Colin and I then put a rope on the stern and began pulling it towards shore. She was taking water pretty fast, I kept watching as the water slowly crept up the legs of the galley table. Finally she slid off some of the cradles and came around pretty close to shore. Thus she was pointing downstream and close to the north shore. Walter and Colin rigged up the rented pump, also our own little pump. Then Colin and I hand operated the bilge pump. Walter was doing yeoman service by plugging leaks with rags and oakum driven into cracks from the inside where water was boiling up. She gradually continued to fill until she rested on some of the timbers which were now in the mud. Colin went to Resolution to get gas and another pump if possible. It was now 11 p.m. and we decided to keep watch for a while yet. It could have been worse. In the meantime I kept wondering when the swelling of the wood hull would come to the rescue. Thinking back to how long it took dried out wooden rain barrels to swell until the iron bands tightened up I made my own estimate of 3 to 4 hours.

Sunday, July 4. This was a continuation of the launch as we did not go to bed. Harry and I had had the foresight to prepare a pail full of boiled brown rice with raisins and had set it on the deck. Whenever some one was hungry they went to the pail and ladled out some rice for themselves. Colin had obtained another pump which we set to pumping and by 2 a.m. the boat was rising and the water was lowering on the kitchen table legs.

A feeling of relief swept over me. We celebrated the launch with a bottle of Canadian Champagne at 4 a.m.

Pumping continued throughout the night. I slept from 4 to 6 a.m. By 7 a.m. she was up to the water line on the starboard side. There were sleeping bodies in broad daylight on the deck and the rice pail was empty.

The time had come for me to leave for Edmonton. Harry and I had breakfast and then I loaded my baggage and departed for home. During the drive I realized that, considering the years that the boat had been blocked up under full exposure to the weather we could not have expected the boat to float upon launching unless we had recaulked the entire hull. And it would have helped if, in our haste, I had not forgotten Russell Denholm's practical suggestion of pre-soaking the hull by putting water in the bilges.

Phase Five: Post Launching, 1971 to 1984

After July 4, 1971, Walter stayed on with Harry to help with the boat. Measures to get the boat operative were quite extensive. Firstly, Harry checked the engine for silt pollution resulting from partial submersion. Fortunately nothing serious was discovered. After an internal clean up of the boat Harry and Walter set about attaching the rudders.

The two rudders each consisted of a wide iron blade suspended on a steel pipe-stem which hung off a bearing attached to the stern of the boat to each side of the tunnel exit. A system of steel cables ran through the boat connected at the inner end to the Captain's wheel and at the outer end to the rudders. The cable system was arranged to provide direct steering, that is, to turn the boat in a certain direction you would turn the wheel in the same manner as you would turn an automobile steering wheel. Initially, of course, the rudder blades were set at neutral, i e., straight back. The stream of water forced out of the tunnel by the ship's propeller impinged upon the blades as soon as they were turned, thereby producing a lateral force on the stern of the boat.

After filling the fuel tank with diesel and pumping up the air tank with compressed air, they were ready to prepare for a trial run. Starting the engine was a matter of carefully following the starting procedure posted in the engine room, as per the next page.

Memorize and Post in Engine Room
STARTING PROCEDURE INSTRUCTIONS
1. TURN CYLINDER LUBRICATING PUMP OVER FOR 30 REVOLUTIONS
CLOSE FUEL VALVES
OPEN COMPRESSION RELEASE VALVES
TURN ENGINE OVER 2 OR 3 TIMES TO PUMP
FUEL OIL OUT OF THE CYLINDER (TURN OVER BY HAND)
AFTER DOING THIS, STOP THE ENGINE AT PISTONS 1 TO 6 PEAK POSITION, THUS MAKING THE ENGINE READY FOR STARTING (1 AND 6 ARE MARKED ON THE ENGINE)

2. CLOSE THE AIR COMPRESSION VALVES
OPEN THE FUEL VALVES
OPEN THE OIL PRESSURE VALVE
LIFT THE FUEL BY-PASS VALVE UP TO ABOVE THE 3RD NOTCH AND/OR PUMP UP TO 1200 LBS. PRESSURE (FUEL PRESSURE)
OPEN THE ENGINE AIR START VALVE
OPEN THE TANK AIR START VALVE
MAKE SURE THE ENGINE IS IN NEUTRAL
SET THE GOVERNOR (SPEED CONTROL) AT THE 3RD OR 4TH NOTCH
HIT THE AIR START LEVER   BANGO
SHE'S RUNNING!!!
CLOSE AIR START VALVE **AT TANK AND RUN AIR COMPRESSOR**

For their first run Harry and Walter decided to move the Sant' Anna out to Resolution. This would be a bit tacky in that Sawmill Channel disappears into Nagle Bay continuing under water as a serpentine channel. Close to shore Nagle bay is extremely shallow so probing as to the location of the deep channel would be performed by sounding with the boat's long pike pole. This was Walter's job while Harry idled the boat along at a dead slow rate. A couple of times she high-centred on a sand bar, however by running the propeller full power in reverse she was freed for another trial. Once deep water was reached they changed to the normal two-man operation with Harry at the helm and Walter in the engine room. At this point communication between Captain and Engine Room was by electric bell signals in accordance with the following schedule:

SIGNALS

Big Dong	Cancel Every Signal Previously Given
One Short	Slow Speed Ahead
One Long	Slow Speed Reverse
Two Shorts	Half Speed Ahead
One Long, Two Shorts	Half Speed Reverse
Two Longs	Stop
Three Shorts	Full Speed Ahead
One Long, Three Shorts	Full Speed Reverse

The remainder of the run to Resolution was across Nagle Bay, around Mission Point and then directly to Resolution Harbour.

The return run was somewhat easier as they had set a marker indicating the outer end of the deep channel. A few more markers were set indicating turns in the underwater channel up to the point where Sawmill Channel enters the Bay.

It wasn't long before an opportunity presented itself for the Sant' Anna to do real work.

The Captain's Course

An Edmonton contractor, Jack McCalder, had been awarded a financial grant to set up a dimension lumber mill in Ft. Resolution to provide employment in the area. Jack's supply of saw logs was located a number of miles up the Slave River from where it divides to enter the delta. Jack approached Harry and asked whether he could tow some log booms from his yard down to Nagle Landing, where Nagle Channel meets Sawmill Channel and which is connected by bush road to Ft. Resolution.

Harry and Walter decided this was worth a try. Jack supplied them with six barrels of diesel fuel which Walter hand pumped into the boat's fuel tank at Nagle Landing. From there they took the boat up Nagle Channel to the Slave and then several miles up the Slave to Jack's yard. Walter recalls that instead of pulling one heavy log boom it was decided to tow a number of smaller booms in line like a line of barges. This is what was done and Harry and Walter completed two trips of some six booms each to Nagle Landing. Walter recalls that the Sant' Anna had lots of power but navigation was a problem because the long line of logs would occasionally snag on obstacles in the stream. Evidently Harry asked Walter to take the helm and Walter is now amazed that, as a nineteen year old, he was able to come through. All the logs were trucked to McCalder's mill.

Before freeze up the mill was in financial difficulty and McCalder was never able to pay Harry anything more than the six barrels of fuel that he had originally contributed.

By November, 1971, the Sant' Anna was frozen in at the edge of the water next to the Mission property site. I was concerned about possible damage at next spring's break up but Harry felt that the channel ice would be the first to thaw and that ice coming down the channel would pass by the boat and this is what happened in the spring of 1972.

My next contact with the boat was in August, 1973, when I took our second son, Raymond, on a vacation trip to visit Harry at the Sant' Anna. We took along our canoe on the car-top carrier. On arriving at Resolution the Mounties recommended that we unload the canoe and baggage at Nagle Landing and they would drive our car back to their yard for safe-keeping. Ray and I reached the Sant' Anna about 3 p.m. and found that Harry's wife Muriel was there with him.

The boat was on shore near water's edge. Harry was in the midst of some repair work that involved jacking up the port side of the boat. He wanted better access to facilitate re-caulking some planks on that side, Ray and I joined in to help for the next couple of days. After that it began to rain and this triggered another dormant project of Harry's.

For some time he had wanted to check the safety of the compressed air tank in the engine room. The maximum safe air pressure for this tank was rated at one hundred seventy five pounds per square inch. A failure of the tank at such pressure would be catastrophic.

To test such a tank in safety one first fills it with water except for a very small volume at the top where there is an access nipple. Then one pumps in air at the access nipple to double the rated pressure, in this case to three hundred fifty pounds per square inch. As water is virtually incompressible and the steel tank virtually rigid, in the event of a failure only a few cubic inches of compressed air is released through the break, not enough to damage the surroundings. The rain promised to provide Harry with the clean water that he needed to fill the tank. After two days of rain we had collected enough. After filling the tank we began to apply air pressure. To do this Harry had only a special one-man piston type hand pump with a plunger less than one square inch in area. In operating the pump by hand we found that the highest pressure that we could achieve was two hundred seventy five pounds per square inch. At that point we accepted this as an adequate test to indicate that the tank was safe.

Ray and I stayed on for a number of days to help Harry carry out preparations for re-launching the boat. Before that could take place I had to return to Edmonton as did Muriel whose family was expecting her. Therefore Harry asked me to take Muriel along, which I did, arriving in Edmonton on August 25, just in time for Muriel to bid farewell to Rob and his wife as they left on vacation.

A fond memory I have of this trip was the pleasure of picking high quality wild berries that grew in profusion on the delta. There were gooseberries, black and red currants and some red raspberries, all matured to full ripeness without disease or worms. The ripe gooseberries were dark red, not green as I had picked them on the prairie as a boy. And, on the rocky areas surrounding the west bay of Burnt Island, the raspberry plants, although of the dwarf size, nevertheless bore regular size raspberries.

Ray stayed on with Harry and the two of them launched the Sant' Anna by themselves. Ray told me there was another episode of pumping out the leakage but this time they had an adequate supply of pumps. Then Harry and Ray repeated the exercise of finding the navigable channel out into Nagle Bay. This time they took the boat into Hay River and left her there in the fall of 1973, mooring her sheltered in one of the storage bays near the Fisheries property. Ray recalls that the lake had been a little rough on the outward journey and that he and Harry had some difficulty in learning to steer the boat.

By the spring of 1974 the Sant' Anna had sunk to deck level in the Fisheries Storage Bay. In the summer of 1974 Harry and Rob raised the boat by pumping her empty of water.

In June of 1975 Harry and I drove to Hay River and found the Sant' Anna in good condition. We moved her into one of the snyes, mooring her with her starboard side almost touching the steep embankment of the snye. Harry's project for this trip was to repair the cooling tubes on the starboard side. These tubes, and a similar pair attached to the port side, were below water level and served as radiators for keeping the engine cool. Although not damaged, the ones on the starboard side had come loose. He devised new anchorages for them.

Because the tubes were below water we decided to tilt the boat until they were exposed. After rigging up an arrangement of greased timbers on the embankment, together with two hawsers for pulling upward on the starboard side, we were able to tilt the boat by pulling with the monkey winch from the top of the embankment. The upper tube was exposed so that we were able to anchor this pipe. After spending the night on the tilted boat we increased the tilt the next day to complete anchoring the second pipe. During all these shenanigans we had daily visits from Rocky Keen, one of the locals who summarized his thoughts by snorting "You guys are just trying to get away from your wives".

Soon the engine was running and Harry decided to invite Ken and Peggy Hunt, Barbara and Bruce together with a visiting couple from Alberta, for a late evening cruise on the lake. We went out about two miles and then returned, giving each of the men a turn at steering the boat. Everything went well and we had everyone home, including ourselves, by dawn about 3:15 a.m.

After a day's recuperation Harry and I decided to go on an outward cruise in the general direction of the MacKenzie River. Our first stop was at the Shell Marine Dock for diesel fuel. After pulling up and stopping the engine we were informed that it was the wrong dock. This meant going through the lengthy sixteen point sequence of restarting the engine which resulted in loud mutterings encouraging us to "Hurry up!"

Under way we decided that Hay River's tallest building, a 12-storey apartment tower, would be our landmark. It was a beautiful June day with a cool breeze towards the bow that reminded us that the water was ice cold.

The Captain's Course

Operating the boat on open water resulted in a learning experience in steering the boat. In the first trial turn one would initially turn the Captain's wheel as one would steer a car. Initially nothing would happen, the boat kept going straight, and the reaction would be to turn the wheel more strongly. Suddenly the boat would swing sharply in the desired direction. Then the reaction was to turn the wheel strongly in the opposite direction. The over-all result was that one would travel forward in a series of decreasing arcs straddling a certain heading:

In a surprisingly short time we learned to turn the wheel cautiously and anticipate the time delay in the boat's reaction. Soon we felt we had the boat fully under control.

We did have the Magnetometer operating on the bow to make this an official search trip. About mid-afternoon the apartment disappeared below the horizon. We estimated we were about 14 miles out so decided to set a return course for Hay River. After three hours we arrived at the outer navigation marker. Upon our return I made a memo of some items that Harry could use on the boat:

The Captain's Course

A marine compass
A digital depth indicator
A Canadian flag
An air whistle

In early October, 1976, Harry and I thought it would be nice to take out the Sant' Anna for another run. I met Harry at the Hay River airport. After coffee we found the Sant' Anna moored in the snye, completely hemmed in by barges. The Northern Transportation Company told Harry they would arrange for a yard boat to come in to clear a passage for us.

As it turned out there simply was no room in any of the other snyes in which to store the barges. The result was we had to cancel our proposed run with the Sant' Anna. As an alternative Harry suggested we drive his car on a holiday trip to Fort Simpson, some two hundred miles down the MacKenzie from the lake. We found this to be a scenic drive, quite carefree for us as compared to searching for Cats.

Just short of Fort Simpson, at the Liard river crossing, we were surprised to encounter John Pope as operator of the ferry across the Liard. Time was too brief to discuss searching for Cats although John did tell us about a D7 Cat that he had raised through the sea ice in the Arctic Islands.

On the return drive we continued to enjoy the scenery and were impressed by the picnic site alongside the Trout River where picnic tables set up at the water's edge could be accessed by automobiles driven onto the exposed stone river bed.

Upon returning to Hay River we spent a couple of days on the Sant' Anna while we helped Ken Hunt pick up gravel with his truck to fill a depression in his drive-way. After that I flew back to Edmonton and Harry drove home with his car.

This marked the end of my visits to the Sant' Anna. However, in 1978, Harry, Muriel, Rob and his daughter Karen spent a pleasant week-long holiday at Burnt Island on the Sant'Anna. Robe recalls that Harry's prime project on the trip was to "Box the Compass", that is, make adjustments to the magnetic compass to cancel out magnetic interferences due to iron on board.

The next spring break-up of the ice on the Hay River was more severe than average, with the result that the build-up of ice and water bulldozed its way across all of the snyes and bodily moved the Sant' Anna high up on the embankment of the most westerly snye. She was deposited in a fairly level orientation in a location where she partially obstructed access to what was called Porritt's Landing. This is where Bobby Porritt and the town planned to develop a small Marina in the snye.

The Captain's Course

While she was up on the embankment someone entered the Bridge of the Sant' Anna and stole the Captain's wheel, cutting it free by sawing through the brass shaft which the wheel turned. This was a blow that hit Harry hard as he felt devastated that someone would ruin the Sant' Anna just to obtain a decoration for a rumpus room.

I believe that Harry knew that the Sant' Anna's days were numbered as he had also noticed that one of the rudders was missing. He was pretty sure it had been torn off by the ice and that it would be in the mud of the embankment.

Earlier Harry's wife Muriel had passed away. As Muriel had stood by Harry so much on his tractor searches and made it possible for him to spend the time on the Sant' Anna, this was a great loss to Harry. I believe her absence dampened his enthusiasm in carrying on with the maintenance of the Sant' Anna.

Perhaps that is why, as winter arrived, he gave permission to two young homeless men when they asked if he would be prepared, in return for them looking after the boat, to let them live in the Galley for the winter. This turned out all right as the men lived there for a few months, the only sign evident being that they had used the stern post as a chopping block.

In the next year, as the Sant' Anna remained on the embankment, Harry, Rob and Colin spent some time digging under the boat so they could set up some jacks under her. They then jacked her up sufficiently to enable them to remove the bronze propeller and the stainless steel propeller shaft.

After that the Sant' Anna remained where she was for several years. She was there in 1984, the year that Harry passed away.

For some time the Town had wanted to burn the Sant' Anna as a project for giving their Fire Department practice to carry out a training burn. As the planning for construction of an access ramp to Porritt's Landing proceeded they asked Ken Hunt to contact Rob Hubbard asking him to grant permission for the Town of Hay River to burn the boat. Rob then sent a letter donating the Sant' Anna to the Town Fire Department. The town then burned the Sant' Anna, but Ken convinced them to let him keep the Capstan as a memento to be placed in the Hay River Museum.

PART SEVEN
One Final Surprise

One day in the early eighties I happened to see a legal notice in the Edmonton Journal placed by lawyer John Kempo on behalf of Claud McDonald. The notice was to the effect that Claud had located a sunken vessel identified as the City of New Orleans on the bottom of Great Slave Lake. I took this to mean that, after many years, Claud had returned to the lake and relocated the boat.

The notice went on to give the location of the sunken vessel by stating the latitude and longitude of the boat. It appears that Claud intended this notice to establish his first right to salvage the vessel.

The figures were stated in degrees and minutes of each of North Latitude and West Longitude. On studying the numbers it was clear to me that they must be erroneous since the stated location was miles and miles from the area where Claud first dropped the boat after raising it in 1960. At that time his efforts had concentrated on dragging the boat to Fort Resolution. This would have been logical in any salvage attempt but the stated location was nowhere near a route to Fort Resolution. I concluded that the latitude and longitude were so erroneous that they would be of no value in re-locating the vessel; therefore I did not bother to keep the advertisement.

With this information we are left with four Caterpillar Tractors and one steel boat named City of New Orleans as a legacy of secrets of the Lake arising from that dangerous storm of July, 1942.

The End

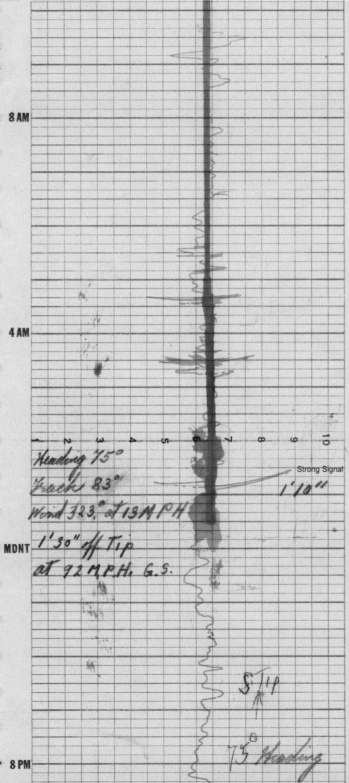

Appendix 1

THE ESTERLINE-ANGUS CO., INC., INDIANAPOLIS

C
O
P
Y

Appendix 2

Steamship Inspector's Office,
Hay River, N.W.T.,
May 20, 1963.

M.V. Santa Anna

Requirements for inspection

1. Master with minor water T.B. masters certificate or Temporary
masters certificate to be in charge.

2. Renew all rotted planks in tunnel - and port and starboard sides.
Renew all short sections of planking (planks not less than 6 ft.
long and no two adjacent butts to be on same frame.

3. Fit W.T. Bulkheads fwd. and aft. of engineroom.

4. Install two bilge pumps one independently driven i.e. (not from
main engine.

   Install bilge suction pipes $1\frac{1}{2}$" dia. suction to each water tight
   compartment - control valves to be in engineroom.

   Connect one pump to sea valves and pipe to deck with sufficient
   hose & nozzle for fire hose to reach any part of vessel.

   Bilge suction valves to be of non-return type or check valve
   fitted so that sea water will not run back through bilge lines.

5. An approved Class I lifeboat to be placed on board with Boom, mast
or davits so that lifeboat can be launched on both sides of
vessel.

   Following equipment required in lifeboat: Bailer, bucket, boat
   hook, oars, rowlocks, steering oar, two plugs, rudder, tiller,
   lifeline around lifeboat, two hatchets, oil and lantern, box
   lifeboat matches in watertight tin, lifeboat compass, sea
   anchor, painter (line attched to stem, 1 gall.wave oil, 12 red
   hand flares).

6. One bouyant apparatus (8 persons)

7. Two approved lifebuoys

8. One approved lifejacket for each person

9. Two anchors - one 250 lb. and one 200 lbs. - withn 45 Fath. 5/8"
chain or wire.

10. Navigation lights to regulations.

11. Two foam (2 gall) or 10 lb. CO_2 or dry chemical extinguisher in
machinery space.

12. One 2 gall. foam or 10 lb. CO_2 or 10 lb. dry chemical extinguisher in galley.

13. One 2 gall. foam or soda acid fire extinguisher in crews accomodation.

14. Three fire buckets, 1 fire axe.

15. vessel to have - fog bell, fog horn, compass.

                                Signed

                                J. Moorcraft,
                                Steamship Inspector.

                                        C
                                         O
                                          P
                                           Y

This Agreement in duplicate prepared this twenty-seventh day of April,

1961, between:

> Decury Supply Ltd., a company duly incorporated under the laws of
> the Province of Alberta with offices at 10330 - 104th Street, in
> the city of Edmonton in the Province of Alberta.
> (hereinafter called the "Owner")

Of the First Part.

And

> Northern Search and Salvage Ltd., a company incorporated under the
> laws of the Province of Alberta, with offices at
>
> in the City of Edmonton, in the Province of Alberta.
> (hereinafter called the "Contractor")

Of the Second Part.

WITNESSETH that whereas

(a) The owner has purchased, where is/as is, the steel barge, built in
     1946 at Vancouver, B.C. and registered at the Port of Vancouver
     under the name of Barge "Y.T.C 103", Official Number 177763, of
     231.53 tons gross, from Yellowknife Transportation Company Limited.

(b) The barge is presently situate at the bottom of Great Slave Lake in
     the Northwest Territories in an undertermined location.

(c) The owner agrees to provide the Contractor with all information
     available to assist in the locating of the sunken barge.

(d) The Contractor agrees to conduct search operations, on a "No cure-
     No pay" basis, for the sunken barge by means of aircraft and electronic
     activities in the area.

(e) The Contractor agrees that in the event the barge is located, positive
     identification will be provided the owner and a marker buoy, designed
     to withstand the break-up of the lake ice, will be attached to the
     barge.

(f) The Contractor further agrees that if the barge is located he will
     then carry out operations to bring the barge to the surface and
     transport it to the shipyard of Yellowknife Transportation Co. Ltd.
     at Hay River, N.W.T.

(g) It is agreed that the fee for locating, raising and moving the barge
     to shore will be $20,000.00, payable as follows:
     (a) Upon completion of work outlined in paragraph (e) above,
         prior to break-up of ice $5,000.00

     (b) Upon re-locating after break-up $2,500.00

     (c) Upon completion of raising and moving barge to dock site
         at Hay River $12,500.00

(h) In the event that barge is located but the owner undertakes the salvage,
     then the fee payable for locating before and after break-up will be
     $10,000.00.

IN WITNESS WHEREOF the parties hereto have affixed their Corporate
seals under the hands of their proper officers this   day of
1961.

The Corporate Seal of the Owner   )
was affixed hereto in the presence of:)
)
)
)
)
The Corporate Seal of the Contractor)
was affixed hereto in the presence of:)
)

Appendix 4

Man on right is Harry Hubbard

Salvaged Cat being driven

Lifting the Mac and Mac Cat

Blasting hole in ice

On the bow of the "Barbara Ann"

Left to right: Pat Kasten, Hector Miron, Cecil Rogers (visiting only), Harry Hubbard, and our magnetometer head.

The Sant' Anna at her final resting place near Porritt Landing

Appendix 5

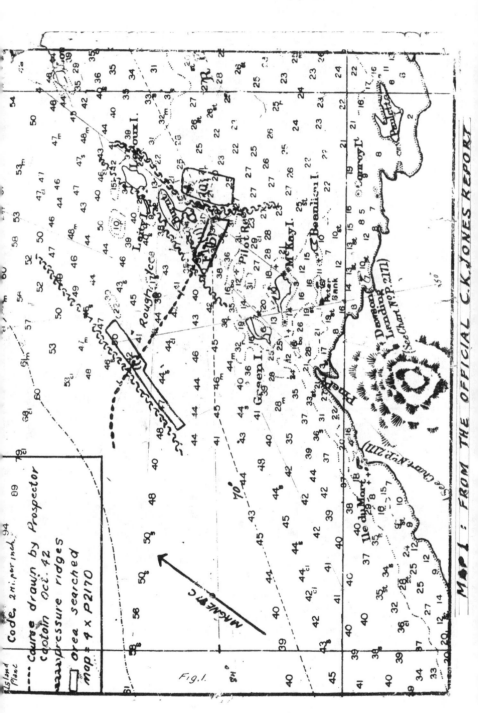

MAP 1: FROM THE OFFICIAL C.K. JONES REPORT

Fig.1.

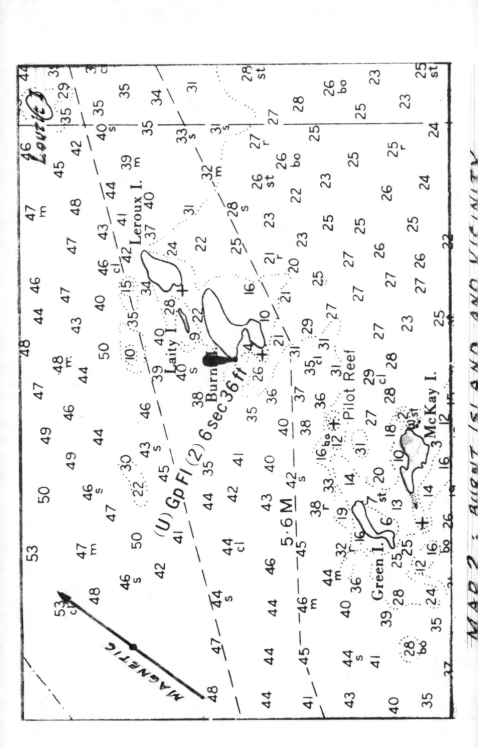

MAP 2 : AUNT ISLAND AND VICINITY

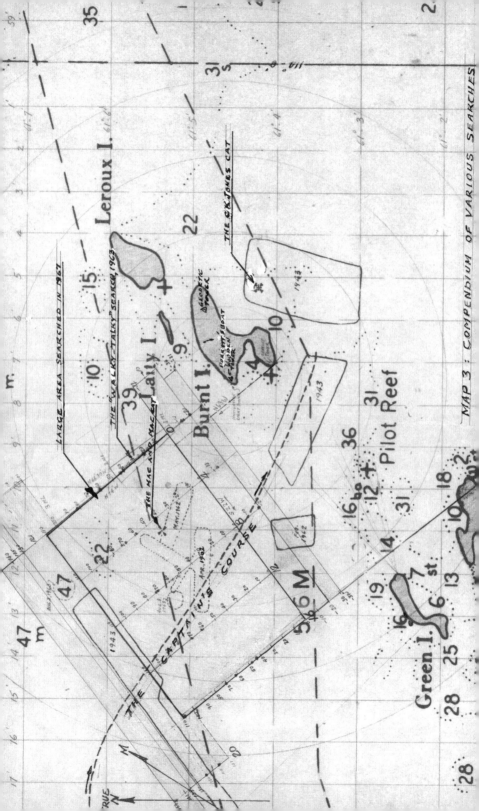

MAP 3 : COMPENDIUM OF VARIOUS SEARCHES

Appendix 6

GLOSSARY OF TERMS

RIGGING EQUIPMENT

> Broad term describing equipment used by trades people ranging from safety harness to heavy industrial lifting devices.

NORTH-WEST STAGING ROUTE

> A line of air-fields constructed by the U.S. Army more or less along the route of the Alaska Highway to serve American war-planes flying to Alaska and eventually to Russia.

BOMBARDIER

> Generally pronounced Bomb-a-Deer. A medium size tracked vehicle for traveling on snow and ice, named after its inventor, also the inventor of the smaller, very popular, snowmobile.

TRIPLE BLOCKS

> Refers to two sets of three pulleys each used with ropes or cables to lift heavy objects.

CANDLING OF ICE

> The formation of large candle-like columnar "crystals" within thick ice when subjected to several

days of sun-driven thawing temperatures. Generally not clearly visible until the ice breaks up.

CABOOSE

A small shack of wooden construction on timber runners for towing on ice. May be equipped with amenities for cooking and sleeping for a small crew.

RIP (As in sawing wood)

To saw along the direction of the grain.

SPILING

A method of determining what length of plank would just fill a curved and twisted gap in a ship's hull.

PORT/STARBOARD

Respectively, left and right sides of a ship as determined when facing from Stern to Bow.

SNYE

An abandoned channel in the delta of a river, filled with water and generally still connected to the main channel of the river. At Hay River Town there were at least three snyes side-by-side.

CAPSTAN

An upright winch, hand operated, on the bow of a boat for raising and lowering the anchor.

FIRE-TUBE BOILER

A type of steam boiler where the heat and flames from the combustion chamber pass through steel tubes to boil water surrounding the tubes until steam forms to accumulate under pressure in a steam chamber.

Appendix 7

TABLE OF SELECTED IMPERIAL/METRIC
EQUIVALENTS

ITEM	Imperial Quantity	Metric Equivalent
Area	32 square Miles	82.9 Square Kilometres
	80 Acres	32.37 Hectares
Distance	1100 Miles	1771 Kilometres
	600 Miles	966 Kilometres
	120 Miles	193 Kilometres
Length	4 to 5 Feet	120 to 150 Centimetres
	500 Feet	152 Metres
	400 Feet	122 Metres
Pressure	275 Pounds per Square inch	1896 Kilopascals
Volume	45 Imperial Gallons	1/5 Cubic Metre
	45 U.S. Gallons	.17 Cubic Metre
Weight	1000 pounds	453.6 Kilograms

Temperature

	40 Below Fahrenheit	Minus 40 Celsius
	43 Below Fahrenheit	Minus 41.6 "
	53 Below Fahrenheit	Minus 47.2 "
	25 Below Fahrenheit	Minus 31.6 "

Appendix 8: Bibliography

1. NATIONAL RESEARCH LABORATORIES, OTTAWA CANADA, DIVISION OF PHYSICS AND ELECTRICAL ENGINEERING REPORT NO. P-85, DATE MAY, 1943: MAGNETIC DETECTION OF LOST OBJECTS, AUTHOR C.K. JONES.

2. ARTICLE, THE BEAVER MAGAZINE, SEPTEMBER 1945 ISSUE, ENTITLED NORTHERN SALVAGE, BY WILLIAM STEPHENSON

3. CANOL, THE SUB-ARCTIC PIPELINE AND REFINERY PROJECT CONSTRUCTED BY BECHTEL, PRICE, CALLAGHAN FOR THE CORPS OF ENGINEERS, U.S. ARMY.

    San Francisco, Bechtel, Price, Callaghan, 1945

    > On page six *"several loads of pipe dropped into the Slave River, and Great Slave Lake claimed half a dozen tractors and a couple of road graders"*.

4. BERTON, PIERRE

    THE MYSTERIOUS NORTH, 1956

    > In Part 1, page 5, mentions being on the lake in August, 1954, and

comments on lost tractors with men on the water searching for them. Later, in PART V makes several comments about sinkings near Burnt Island, including a cabin cruiser. Also refers to an unmarked reef

5. HURSEY, ROBERTA L

TRUCKING NORTH ON CANADA'S MACKENZIE HIGHWAY, 2000

- Chapter 3 gives a good overview account of the Canol Project.
- Throughout the book numerous references to Earle Harcourt comprise a biographical history of this northern entrepreneur in outline form.

6. CANADIAN HYDROGRAPHIC SERVICE

NAVIGATION MAP, GREAT SLAVE LAKE, SLAVE RIVER TO MACKENZIE RIVER AND RAE, CORRECTED REPRINT NOV. 3, 1961 OF NEW EDITION, 1958

Invaluable to searchers of sunken equipment.